D0949833

THE
MENDER'S
MANUAL

By the same author: "SIX CHILDREN," the findings of Dr. Foote's school clinic in Massachusetts, for children having difficulties with the school curriculum.

THE MENDER'S MANUAL

Repairing and preserving garments and bedding

ESTELLE FOOTE, M.D.

Harcourt Brace Jovanovich

 New York and London

Printed in the United States of America

Library of Congress Cataloging in Publication Data
Foote, Estelle J
    The mender's manual.
    Includes index.
    1. Clothing and dress—Repairing. I. Title.
TT720.F66   646.4   76-12102
ISBN: 0-15-159150-4

First edition

B C D E

OUR FOREFATHER'S SONG_____-

Excerpt from a poem composed about 1630 by one of the forefathers, author unknown.

> And now our garments begin to grow thin,
> And wool is much wanted to card and to spin;
> If we can get a garment to cover without,
> Our other in garments are clout* upon clout;
> Our clothes we brought with us are apt to be torn,
> They need to be clouted soon after they're worn,
> But clouting our garments they hinder us nothing.
> Clouts double, are warmer than single whole
>   clothing.

* Clout signifies patching

Courtesy of the Massachusetts Historical Society

CONTENTS

6 OTHER PROBLEMS 147

THE PRAISE OF THE NEEDLE 179

LIST OF ILLUSTRATIONS

PREFACE_____

When cloth was hand spun and hand woven and correspondingly scarce and dear, the ability to do skillful mending was well appreciated. Poets even wrote of it. Three centuries ago, John Taylor, in a long and famous poem about needlework, part of it celebrating English queens as needleworkers, included words of praise for the needle that was also "a mender." Then spinning and weaving machinery were invented, cloth became cheaper and more plentiful and, somehow, regard for mending as an art lessened.

Now, again, hand skills are becoming more highly regarded and the person, usually the housewife, who can do neat, and sometimes beautiful, mending, can expect appreciation and admiration.

This book was written to describe the best and quickest ways to mend clothing. It also would like to show you that you can find mending an interesting as well as a rewarding occupation. We found it could be and I am sure you can. The original "we" was a small mending committee, of which I was chairman, part of a larger group organized to help underprivileged folk, chiefly by collecting and giving out good used clothing.

Understandably, we became more and more expert menders as we benefited from the comments and suggestions of the recipients of the mended clothing. We did not need to be told that care and attention to the appearance of the mended garments would be appreciated.

While we zealously mended, I tried to find books

and articles on mending aids and ways to solve today's problems, for we needed help. I found very little; we had to figure out ways to mend the clothing ourselves.

I started this book to put on record the methods worked out, to aid our successors or other groups doing similar work. Then, thinking it over, I rewrote it for general use. In the course of my rewriting, I did some research in such things as today's man-made threads and fashions, the modern sewing machine's variations and attachments, and mending gadgets old and new. I tried to cover the field and find any useful ideas that my personal experience, even though it covered nine years of welfare mending, might not have given me.

I want to express my gratitude to Edith Willis, Mary Carpenter and Dorothy Spooner, who put this manuscript into working order in my nephew's law office; to the librarians at the Ilsley Library, who sent for books for me; to Mr. and Mrs. Robert Drake, who aided in locating gadgets I needed; to Connie Schrader, my editor at Harcourt Brace Jovanovich; and especially to my faithful co-worker, Kathleen Kent, who is also Mrs. Rockwell Kent.

1

GENERAL NOTES

Mending partakes more of the nature of embroidery than it does of ordinary sewing. Indeed, often the stitches that you mend with are embroidery stitches. And mending calls for the same qualities in a person that embroidery does: ingenuity, good judgment, some skill and dexterity. It is challenging.

In ordinary sewing, such as making a garment, you buy a pattern and some material and follow the printed directions, usually making only a few or no adaptations. It has relatively little demand on your resourcefulness. Then someday you are called on to mend that garment and an entirely different set of abilities is called for. For the mending of weakened, worn, torn or ragged material can be done in many ways: by darning, by stitching open edges together, by ironing on prepared patches or by sewing or cementing (with fabric cement) the material to a patch. Each method has its virtue, depending on the value or use or condition of the article to be mended and sometimes according to the ability, the time available or even the mood of the mender.

Consider Each Problem You consider each mending problem. How much useful wear is left in this garment? One general rule is that if six months' wear is left in it, it is probably worth mending. However, a child's warm winter coat may be worth mending for three months of winter wear, and the baby's rompers, mended quickly and firmly but with less than the usual regard for appearance, may be worth mending for an even shorter period of time. One mends a cheerful red plaid shirt when one wouldn't bother to mend a dull greenish one, for everyone likes a red plaid blouse in cold weather.

Use Imagination You should not be too easily satisfied with a "homemade-looking" mend in a good outside garment. Cement a small colorful appliqué over a mend on the front of a child's dress. Consider matching a new seam or a patch-disguised-as-a-pocket on one side of a garment by one on the other, and let the beholder try to puzzle out for himself why the manufacturer put them on that way.

Be on the lookout for ideas on covering up mends. This is especially to be kept in mind when you have children's clothing to mend. You see a blouse with epaulettes, for instance; it may help you to contrive a mend for a pulled-apart shoulder seam. Look over the findings in notions departments. They may have mending gadgets you never thought of. If you find a knowledgeable clerk, tell her of your problem and ask her if she has anything that might help. Look for ideas on the streets, in the playground and, surreptitiously, at more exclusive gatherings.

Thread When doing mending in which stitches will show on the surface of the cloth, you strive to make your stitches as inconspicuous as possible—even, sometimes, to the extent of using, for hand mending, threads taken from the material being mended.

Use, for ordinary mending, thread that matches the material as accurately as possible, or a thread a shade darker. A useful alternative, if you are a person who doesn't have room, or desire, for many spools of many colors in your workbasket, is to use transparent nylon thread for machine sewing when the stitches will show on the surface of the material. For stitching on dark material, there are dark single-filament threads available. (When you go to purchase transparent nylon thread, be sure that is exactly what you get; a *white* nylon thread may be there, and it is not transparent.)

Threading the machine is not difficult when you can see the thread. Try turning on the sewing machine light, even if it is broad daylight. This seems to show up the thread as darker than it actually is.

If the wiry nylon thread resists being wound onto the bobbin (and it can resist quite fiercely), fasten the end of the thread onto the hub of the bobbin with a bit of scotch tape.

Once the machine is threaded with the slender wiry thread, you can stitch about on all colors and materials, and on most it hardly shows. Also, it wears well and does not shrink. One care must be taken: do not iron it with a hot iron. Use only a warm iron on nylon.

For hand sewing, again, that transparent or dark nylon thread is to be used when you do not want your stitches to show on the surface. For other hand stitching, a multi-filament nylon thread is more supple and easily managed. Do not try to use the multi-filament thread on the sewing machine; the filaments break and form a fluffy mass which clogs the needle.

In the hand, single-filament nylon thread needs care in its management. It is very difficult to tie a knot in the end of the thread. Instead, take several tiny stitches in the cloth, trying to form a knot there. Also, the wiry thread wants to catch on every pin or even on a corner of the cloth.

It is worthwhile to practice until you have mastered the art of sewing with nylon thread, in the hand and on the machine. It takes some time, and a sense of humor, to fight it out, but if you do, sometimes you can make an almost invisible mend with your almost invisible thread that seems like magic.

In machine stitching, nylon thread tends to pucker any but heavy or wiry cloth. Working with thread of ordinary thickness, if you do not put it in an embroidery frame you must loosen the tension and pull the cloth away from you as you stitch. Finally, it is hard to describe your feelings—admiration and exasperation mixed—when you find you can't be sure whether the stitches are catching each other and stitching or not, this nylon stitching is so transparent and sometimes so well hidden.

It was at first only amusing to read, in two books which included some advice on mending, the suggestion that human hairs could be used to achieve almost invisible mends. If you try it, however, you will find that human hairs do work well. If hair of suitable color is used, it is as invisible as single-filament nylon, and it is less wiry than nylon and consequently a little easier to manage. Like nylon, it is difficult to knot at the end, but, again, you can stitch a tiny knot in the cloth. Of course, for invisible machine mending, you need the continuous nylon thread from the spool.

You will require some spools of ordinary thread. The most useful colors to have on hand for mending, after black and white, are bright red, navy blue and, especially, shades of gray or gray-green. Gray is a useful color for the mender, for the clothes she mends are often more or less faded and the grayish thread harmonizes with them better than does bright-colored thread. You will be surprised and pleased at the usefulness and versatility of your gray threads.

The threads are all usually available in size 50, which is a good all-round size.

Does your thread sometimes tie itself in little looped knots as you hand sew? Do as your great-grandmother did—wax your thread. She used beeswax, pulling it easily along her thread. A little ball of paraffin will do as well, though it lacks the hint of fragrance possessed by the traditional wafer of beeswax.

Needles For your hand sewing, look thoroughly over the types of needles available, not only at notion counters but also in the small specialty stores found in large cities and sometimes where quantities of yard goods are sold. Note the size of the needle, the size of the eye, the length of the needle and the sharpness of the point. In-betweens are shorter than the average. Select the ones that suit you best.

Standard advice is to use, for everyday sewing, #7 or #8 needles. Investigate embroidery and crewel needles, which have large eyes. (Fig. 1.) They are

Embroidery and crewel needles

1

easy to thread (and some of us have less clear vision as we grow older) and they take more easily the large threads, such as darning cotton, embroidery floss and wool thread. The various kinds of needle threaders (Fig. 2), which can be bought in specialty stores, only work with large-eyed needles.

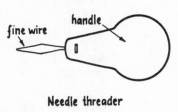

Needle threader

2

Shears Get a pair of really good, sharp shears, of standard make, preferably the kind that has its cutting edge inlaid with especially hard steel. You can make these do for almost all your mending needs. If you have a job that absolutely requires pinking shears, take your work to a friend who has a pair and see if she will let you use hers for a few minutes; this isn't too much to ask.

A minor frustration of a mender's existence, and one that sometimes doesn't seem very minor either, is to have shears grow dull. A real improvement of modern life has been the recent proliferation of places where shears, including pinking shears, can be quickly and competently resharpened. (Has the machinery for this just been put on the market?)

Gadgets When doing handwork, you will find it a convenience to have one end of the work firmly clamped to something. Our foremothers used "sewing birds," which you may have seen in antique shops. (Fig. 3.) The working parts of a sewing bird are: a

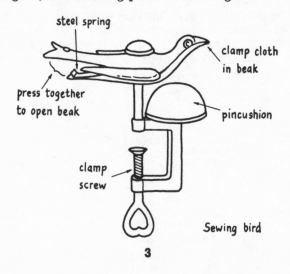

steel spring

clamp cloth in beak

press together to open beak

pincushion

clamp screw

Sewing bird

3

clamp that screws onto the edge of a table or shelf (sewing tables of a century and a half ago might have a little shelf at the back just for this) and a little metal bird whose beak would firmly clasp onto the end of the cloth when body and tail were pinched together. You can still obtain inexpensive modern copies. You can also make a substitute with a snap clothespin, securing it to a table corner by a small screw clamp.

Look for other useful gadgets at notion counters, in stores that sell yard goods and in stores that sell sewing machine attachments (of which more later). Be open-minded—you may find gadgets that you used to know now dressed in new guises, as in plastic instead of in metal, and under new names, as "pull-throughs" instead of "bodkins." (Fig. 4.)

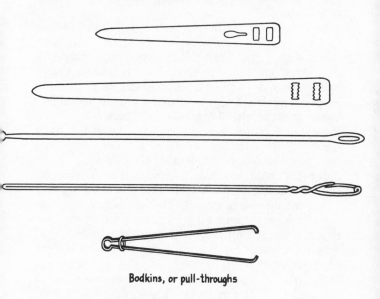

Bodkins, or pull-throughs

4

When doing fine handwork, you may feel the need of a magnifying glass. Forms of holders for such a magnifying glass have been devised which are very convenient for the needleworker; you can look through the glass at your work but your hands are free. One form is designed for your table. Another rests loosely on your chest, the glass held so you can see through it by a cord that goes around your neck. Try one before you buy it, and get the one that is right for you.

If you have a needed gadget in mind that the stores do not seem to have, ask about it. They may have a gadget that you had not known of which can make an effective substitute. Don't depend on books to tell you of all the things useful for mending that can be found in the stores; by the time a book is on sale, still more newly invented gadgets may be available to you.

In the course of the research I had instituted, to find all possible good ways to mend and things to mend with, I had the strange experience of finding that some appliances, yarns, even materials that I had once used, handled or at least known of were no longer available. There had been a narrow metal embroidery hoop, with flanges on the inside hoop, made to hold cloth (and to hold some of it out of the way) for machine darning. Another, smaller hoop had curved loops that could hold a rolled-up sock so the foot parts could be machine darned. The mushroom-shaped darner, with its metal hoop around the top of the mushroom is extinct. The last blow—with entire confidence I entered a yarn shop and asked for elastic yarn, to knit fresh wristlets for windbreakers, only to be told, "Yes, we once had that yarn but we can't get it any more."

Elastic   Elastic in various forms is often useful to mend with. It can replace tapes, which give way, and can make a garment more comfortable to wear; elastic cord can provide a "give" that makes it easy to slip over a button.

When stitching elastic to knit material, whether hand knit or machine knit, remember to stretch the elastic and material as you stitch it. If your machine has a zigzag-stitching attachment, use it for sewing over elastic and other stretch material.

Doubled elastic may make a rather thick and bunched place when stitched; sometimes you can sew the two ends side by side instead of over each other, making a V. You can then attach the hook or whatever to the folded end. (Fig. 5.)

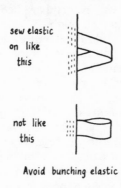

sew elastic on like this

not like this

Avoid bunching elastic

5

When you are replacing a spent elastic band with a fresh one, use the old elastic to pull the new one through the casing. Find the seam in the casing, snip one stitch and pull the opening wide enough to slip something under the old elastic and pull some of it out. At once place two medium-sized safety pins in this spent elastic and cut between the pins. The safety pins are there to ensure that those two ends do not pull back into the casing.

Sew an end of your new elastic to an end of the old. Take out that safety pin and use the other end of the old elastic to pull the new elastic into the casing. Again, while you prepare to sew the two ends of the new elastic together, place a safety pin in each end. The fresh elastic is even more prone than the old to snap out of sight into the casing. Last, sew up the seam you snipped in the casing.

You run an elastic through an empty casing, of course, with a safety pin or bodkin. If you buy a bodkin, you will find it amusing to see all the kinds available in a well-stocked specialty store. A useful bodkin is not too wide, not too altogether long, and has a large eye. And remember, bodkins are now sometimes called "pull-throughs."

Fabric Cement   Fabric cement deserves a full explanation, for you will find it a very useful aid. You buy it in tubes, usually at notion counters. Unfortunately, they contain, too often, large amounts of air. Look closely at the guarantee on the card; it should read, "Resistant to washing," or "Holds even after washing and dry cleaning," or wording that gives the same guarantee. Fabric cements that do not hold after washing are not worth buying.

When cementing a large patch, apply the cement in a band around the edge, not all over it; this seems to hold well.

Opening Seams   For one reason or another, you will often want to open seams, or to open up "pulled" seams more widely. You will find that I use the word "snip" for a seam that is to be opened, suggesting the use of scissors, which is the safer method. Those of us who are sure-fingered or can stand getting little cuts occasionally can use razor blades (the one-sided kind, or with one sharp side covered with adhesive). Do you know you can resharpen them, well enough to use for seam ripping, on a fine whetstone or on fine emery paper?

Whenever you plan to take out a seam in a purchased article, see if it was sewed by "chain stitch," which is a single thread looped into a chain. If it was, with your embroidery scissors loosen or cut the thread at the end toward which the loops point, and you may be able to get the seam out quickly and painlessly with long pulls.

Chain stitching occurs more often than you would expect. Manufacturers use it, for economy, to sew seams that are not under strain. The operator of a chain-stitch machine uses but the one long thread and saves time by not having to stop to put in fresh bobbins, as the worker on the two-thread machine must do.

The Home Dressmaker   The problems of mending are lessened for the person who sews and knits for the family. The left-over cloth, yarn and buttons can come in handy; non-washable fabrics, for instance, usually have not faded enough to show up the freshness of a small inset patch. How to meet the problems of mending with left-over yarn will be taken up in the section "Knit Materials."

Read This Book Through First   All the available advice about any mending problem you may have may not be found under that one section heading. If you look in "Children's Clothing," for instance, you need to also read, at least, "General Notes," "Repairing Seams," "Cuffs" and "Zippers." In fact, it is advisable to read, or at least glance through, the whole book before starting any mending project.

Useful Publications   Directions are not given in this book for complicated sewing procedures and projects, as to do so would make this a much longer book. Excellent directions, with the necessary drawings and diagrams, can be found in standard books on sewing, available at your library. Even better, purchase for yourself one of the sewing books put out, often in magazine form, by women's magazines and pattern companies. You can seldom buy so much useful information for so relatively little.

It will help to buy, also, a book or pamphlet or article on embroidery stitches, with the needed diagrams and instructions. Some are not expensive and it is more convenient than you may realize, when you want to make use of a certain stitch or method, to have your book of reference right at hand.

Prevention Finally, a word is in order about preventing the needs of mends. When you buy a garment, tug at each button and resew it if it is insecure. Examine any place where two seams meet; there is almost always increased strain at such a location. Examples are: under the arm, in the crotch and at the place where the shoulder seam meets the collar (especially a point of danger in a knitted garment). If any of these places starts to give way at any time, do a careful repair and reinforcement. If you do not—if you try to catch the edges with careless stitches, and these in turn give way, you will finally have to take out the original mending as well as make a fresh one. This will be especially difficult if your first, careless mending was done on the machine, and the complications will be doubled if you stitched it with your zigzagger.

The winters here in Vermont are always cold and sometimes colder. There is more or less snow, more or less wind. We mend windbreakers and their hoods. We mend strong winter pants. We make scarves to twine about our throats and pull up over our chins when we face the wind. We mend mittens.

We mend!

2

FUNDAMENTALS OF MENDING

THE SEWING MACHINE
PATCHES
DARNED MENDS
REPAIRING SEAMS

THE SEWING MACHINE_____

Do as much of your mending as you can on your sewing machine. Not only will you save a great deal of time, you will be surprised to find how often the mending is stronger and better-looking.

Zigzag stitching is useful for sewing on knitted fabrics, such as sewing patches on underwear. In other places in this book, you will find other specialized machine stitching, using sewing machine attachments already spoken of, as the zipper presser foot for zipper stitching and the buttonholer.

It could be an advantage to the mender to have access occasionally to a free-arm sewing machine. (Fig. 6.) In this machine, the mechanism that con-

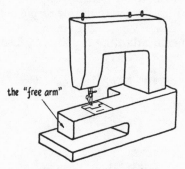

the "free arm"

Free-arm sewing machine

6

tains the bobbin, in its rotary holder, is housed in a thick bar that stands out over the base. A sleeve or pant leg can be slipped right over this bar, facilitating stitching on those parts of a garment. A free-arm machine is not a necessity; the mender can always snip open the inner seam of the arm or leg and flatten the material out to stitch on it, then turn the extremity inside out and restitch the seam.

• Machine Darning

Machine darning is so very useful, all people who sew should secure the appropriate attachments and learn to use them. The mends in this book are planned to be, if humanly possible, permanent ones; you want them to last as long as the garment itself. To accomplish this, often the mend should be reinforced by machine stitching in the form of machine darning.

To do any form of machine darning, you may need to alter somewhat your ordinary method of machine sewing.

General Directions All authorities agree, that unless the material on which you are working is so strong and firm it can't wrinkle or pucker you should stretch it in a strong, tight embroidery frame while you are machine darning it. (Fig. 7.) Use, if possible,

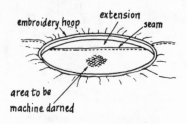

Extension in embroidery hoop

7

a frame with narrow hoops, for it is difficult to get wide hoops under the presser foot. Put the material in the frame wrong side up, so to speak; the cloth must be down on the cover plate, the hoops above, which is not the way you put it in when hand embroidering. If you do not stretch lighter materials in a frame, the stitching will tighten and pucker the darn in a most disfiguring manner.

If you are mending near an edge, sew a piece of cloth along the edge as a temporary enlargement, so that the mending area is equally stretched from all sides when put into the embroidery frame.

Hold the embroidery frame with both hands.

Don't stitch too fast.

Use a finer needle and thread on thinner fabrics and a heavier needle (but not necessarily a much heavier thread) on heavier fabrics.

Reduce the needle thread tension, and sometimes the bobbin thread tension as well. You will almost certainly need to loosen at least the needle thread tension if you are stitching on man-made fabrics, such as Dacron or nylon.

Never start with the needle in mid-air or the thread may break. Take a stitch in the cloth and pull the threads up out of the way, lest you catch the threads in your work.

The Mechanisms If your machine has the reverse-stitching mechanism, you can often do good machine darning with only this, changing the position of the material by a quarter circle if you need to do crosswise stitching as well as front and back.

Real machine darning, using machine darning attachments, enables you to go all over the area to be darned, sidewise and about as well as back and forth, and, usually, to see just where each stitch is being placed. (Fig. 8.)

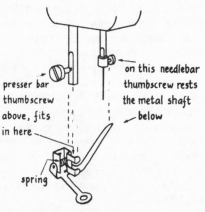

presser bar
thumbscrew
above, fits
in here

on this needlebar
thumbscrew rests
the metal shaft
below

spring

Presser bar, needlebar and
darning foot

8

Begin by eliminating the action of the "feed dog" (also called the "fabric feed"). The feed dog consists of the little corrugated bars running in slots in the needle plate. It rises and falls and moves the cloth forward as you stitch. To eliminate its action, you either lower the feed dog below the level of the needle plate, which is the usual method, or, in some machines, raise the needle plate. The instruction booklet for your machine tells you how to do it; the method varies on different machines but the parts you use are usually well illustrated and marked in the booklets.

Next, remove the ordinary, or "general purpose" presser foot. It is possible to darn without any presser foot at all, and some prefer this. If you do, remember always to lower the presser foot bar. The lever alters the tension, and if it is not lowered, the stitch will loop and make knots underneath. I myself did not find it easy to darn without a spring darning foot. The needle, coming up through the cloth, pulls the cloth up, and I had to press down on the embroidery hoops to keep the cloth down against the needle plate.

The spring darning foot, of which there are several forms, has, ordinarily, three integral parts.

First, in place of the wide presser foot, the spring darning foot has a small loop to rest on the cloth. The person sewing can see just where each stitch is being placed, a necessity in good darning. This loop is at the lower end of a metal shaft, sometimes round, sometimes flat, the upper end of which is a projection that rests on the top of the needlebar.

Second, there is another, separate metal part, which is shaped to go on the lower end of the presser bar, just as your general purpose presser foot was, and is to be fitted into place there.

Third, there is a strong spring, one end of which is attached to the metal shaft somewhere between the loop at the lower end and the bar at the top. The other end of the spring is firmly fixed to the presser bar part just described.

The process, then, is this: the needle comes down, goes through the loop and pierces the cloth. After piercing the cloth, the needle descends further and engages the shuttle, then rises from the shuttle and lifts from the cloth. As it rises, the bar, whose extremity rests on the needlebar thumbscrew, of course also rises, and the lifting bar, working against the spring, causes the looped part of the darning foot to rise, momentarily, from the cloth on which it rested. While it is thus lifted, the cloth can be moved about, as much or as little as one chooses, until the needle descends and the darning foot presses the cloth again. This is the main action of the machine darning mechanism on a modern machine.

Books that deal with "free hand" or "free motion"

machine embroidery can give you helpful advice on the use of the spring darning foot, since the same methods and gadgets used for machine darning are used for this type of machine embroidery. Embroiderers do not seem to think it always necessary to use the spring darning foot; they may only remove the general purpose presser foot, lower the presser foot bar and work with no presser foot of any kind there. Lowering the presser foot bar is a necessity; this procedure creates a certain tension here, which prevents little loops from forming as the needle goes back and forth through the cloth.

Books for "free hand" or "free motion" embroidery are likely to be English; American machine embroidery seems to be mainly zigzag and "cam" stitches, which require very different gadgets and mechanisms.

Pressure Regulator   There is another and entirely different method for machine darning. It is to be used on a sewing machine that has a pressure regulator. (Fig. 9.) Not all machines have them.

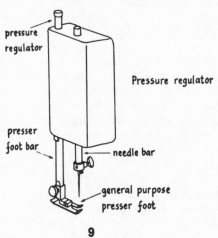

9

After you have disposed of the feed dog's action by lowering it, you loosen the pressure regulator, thus lessening the downward pressure of the ordinary presser foot, and by that means making it possible to move the cloth about under the needle.

The pressure regulator, when present, is at the upper end of the bar that ends below in the presser foot bar. It projects up through the top of the machine. Your instruction manual will tell you how to loosen it, by unscrewing it or by operating a snap lock there at the top of the machine.

It is true that after loosening the pressure regulator you can, more or less, move the cloth about, but most of us prefer to remove and replace the general purpose presser foot rather than to try to regulate it.

Sewing Machine Attachments With today's sewing machines come a number of attachments, most of which the mender may or may not make much use of. The darning foot, which can be one of the most useful of sewing tools, is not often, or not usually, included. It can, however, be easily obtained, from the store from which the sewing machine was purchased or even, if necessary, from the company that manufactured it. It is not at all expensive.

If you do this, be sure to send all the information needed, and especially the model and serial number of your machine. The number or numbers they will need are impressed, as if with a typewriter, into a small metal plate that is attached somewhere on your machine. (Sometimes it is well hidden, under the edge of the machine or, on an older machine, under the attached motor.) Don't try to write the manufacturer without that number. If you send it, even if your machine is an older one, they may be able to help you. Without it, one can almost guarantee that they will only write back to you asking for that vitally necessary model and serial number.

Can you secure modern attachments even if yours is an older machine? It is certainly worth trying.

If you live where there are stores that advertise "Sewing Machine Service" and "Parts for All Machines," that is the first place to look for help. If it appears that no darning foot was made by the manufacturer of your machine, see if there is not some other sewing machine that has a presser bar shaped like yours. There are several makes of sewing machines having similar presser bars, and their attachments can be used interchangeably. All the attachments have to do is fit that shape of presser bar.

"Sales and Service" stores have catalogues from manufacturers of general and special sewing machine attachments. They can ascertain which sewing machines have presser bars similar to that on your machine and whether there exists anywhere an attachment such as you want to fit your machine.

Be warned: you may receive less than enthusiastic co-operation when you ask about these appliances just described. Such stores usually exist to sell sewing machines, and when you ask for attachments to bring your machine up-to-date, you are almost certain to be told, and told, and *told* that you should buy a new machine instead. You may need persistence and, perhaps, a great deal of patience.

It is said that nearly all the imported machines have similar presser bars. Such presser bars are partly flattened at their lower ends and have a thumbscrew there to hold the bent slotted arm of the attachment. One housewife actually had the entire presser bar of her old machine (circa 1917) removed and replaced by one of these modern presser bars, whose lower end was shaped to receive the attachments most commonly available today. (Her engineer-husband made the change.)

If you secure a darning foot for your older ma-

chine, remember that the older machine will probably also lack the mechanism to eliminate the
inexorable forward march of the feed dog. In place
of such a mechanism, you can purchase a "feed
cover plate" to put over the feed dog. For each machine, secure just the right cover plate, for the
screw that holds it in place must go in the hole in
the sewing machine at just the right distance from
the needle.

For an older machine, you will be able to get a
buttonholer and a zigzagger, but for a darning foot
sometimes only an odd little coil of wire that slips
around the needlebar and the needle. This works
fairly well, once you get used to it. With it, you can
use the cover plate that came with the buttonholer
to cover the feed dog. (Fig. 10.)

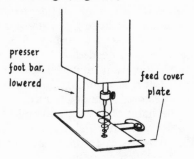

presser
foot bar,
lowered

feed cover
plate

Feed cover plate and
wire-coil darning foot

10

PATCHES_____

Sooner or later you will need patches. We are told
that patching to hide a flaw may have been one of
the origins of the ornamentation of garments. Italian

women of long ago are credited with putting "glorious patches" over tears and mends of fine garments.

In general, do not be too quick to buy new material or ornaments with which to mend an older garment. Too often you find the mended garment, in the end, not worth the cost of the mending material you purchased.

There are exceptions, as buying a new set of buttons when one is lost from a used but still worthwhile coat. You will add, buying ironed-on patches, but don't buy them—use fabric cement for those patches.

When patching any figured material, whether of stripes, plaids or prints (or damask, etc.), if you can secure enough of the material to match the figure accurately, you may be able to make an especially satisfactory mend. One woman has recorded that whenever she made her little girl a dress, she tacked a piece of the material somewhere inside it, to use as a patch if one were ever needed.

But you don't have any material, old or new, for your patching? Get it at rummage sales, garage sales, Salvation Army stores, Goodwill outlets, and from friends with the habit of saving and collecting (who are usually older women). Relatives who live in the country have more room to save and farm women always save materials for patching.

Remember that patching material for washable garments often needs to be shrunk and sometimes even faded before it is used. If the patch should shrink after being put in, it would pucker the already washed material to which it was sewed. One is irresistibly reminded of the Biblical warning against putting unshrunk cloth on an old garment, as well as new wine in old wineskins.

To fade the patch, expose it to the sun or carefully soak it in weak bleaching solution.

We have, in general, three kinds of patching: first, a patch placed under the hole in the material, which is then sewed down to it; second, a patch applied, by whatever means, on the surface, over the hole; third, a patch that is neither of these—it is on the same level as the rest of the material, being painstakingly sewed into its substance. This last is called the inset patch.

Underneath Patch If you have a tear in a work apron, you use an underneath patch, usually. (Fig. 11a.) If the tear is quite irregular (perhaps it was burnt instead of torn), cut back the irregular edges, making it more or less a rectangle. Your cuts should follow the "straight of the goods"—that is, they should be made along the lines of the weave.

Secure a patch the right size, of washed and shrunk material that matches the apron material as well as possible in color, thickness and strength. The best source of the patch here may be an apron pocket. Pockets are among the most common sources of patch material and are among the best. On aprons, they can be replaced by fresh pockets of harmonizing or, often even better, contrasting material.

Pin or baste the patch in place underneath the tear, being sure the "straight of the goods" (that is, the line of the weave) is the same in each. Turn under the torn edge of the apron a very little, perhaps three-eighths of an inch, and hand hem down the torn apron edges to the patch. (Fig. 11b.) Take

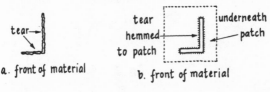

a. front of material

b. front of material

11

the apron to your sewing machine and stitch across the hemmed edges, back and forth, the lines of stitching not very close to each other. (Fig. 11c.) Use matching thread if you have it, but if you do not, on almost any apron white thread will do.

Turn the apron over and cut back the patch edges a half inch to an inch from the stitching, using pinking shears if you have them. Catch down the raw

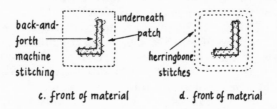

c. front of material   d. front of material

edges of the patch to the apron with stitches that go back and forth, crossing each other; take first a back stitch in the material, then in the patch, across the edges of the patch. Where the stitches catch in the garment material they should be short and fine. (Figs. 11d, e.) Such stitching, crossing over the

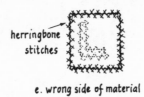

e. wrong side of material

Underneath patch

patch edges, is called in embroidery books "herringbone stitch." In sewing books it is more often called "catch stitch." (Fig. 12.)

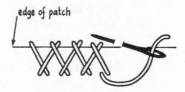

Herringbone, or catch, stitch

12

The Applied Patch We begin by considering the place, probably a worn or torn hole, to be patched. If the material around the hole is stretched and gaping, it would be advisable to draw the stretched edges back into something of their original position before placing a patch over them. With a large round hole, this can be done by running a gathering stitch, by hand, about the edges. With an irregular hole, the edges may be drawn more closely together by stitches across the parts of the hole.

You often meet this problem when you need to mend the knees in workmen's or small boys' pants. Mend them with cemented-on patches. Turn the pants inside out and put on a small patch, just large enough to cover the tear or hole, on the inside first, so that the wearer will not catch his toes in the hole.

For the usual cemented-on patch, you use firm material that is not very thin, for the cement soaks through thin material and shows as a dark, shiny line. Cut your patch, sometimes no larger than a small coin for a very small hole and sometimes several inches across for a knee patch, apply the cement generously about the edges of the wrong side of the patch and place it exactly where you want it to go; if you have to lift it from its first placement, you will have to reapply the cement. Press them firmly together.

Thin patches are much more difficult to keep in place than are thick patches, but with some finger pressure and recementing of the edges here and there, it can be done.

If one side of your cemented-on patch comes against a seam, consider snipping the seam open and including that edge of the patch in it when you resew the seam. Do the same when the worn or torn place you are patching is close to a pocket. Snip loose the pocket where it is adjacent to the patch, push that side or corner of the patch up under the pocket and restitch the pocket over it.

After cementing a patch on, leave the repaired garment alone for at least a couple of hours. It will be ready for wear in twenty-four hours.

There may be times when you want to use a cemented-on patch but wish it to appear stitched on. Simply run a line of stitching about the edge of your patch before you cement it on.

There are times when work pants are to be stitched, not cemented. The knees of work pants, and sometimes of small boys' pants, can often be well and unobtrusively mended, if you can secure accurately matching material—one thinks of the omnipresent blue denim—by opening the side seams, stitching the patch to the knee area above and below the worn place, and then including the sides of the patch in the restitched side seams of the pants. (Fig. 13.)

Leather is useful patch material for good clothing. You can mend sport clothing, as well as clothing that only partly qualifies as sport clothing, with leather—thick or thin, depending on the use of the

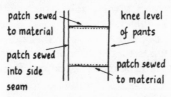

Knee patch sewed into side seams

13

garment. You probably know of leather patches on the elbows of men's heavy sport sweaters. Leather can also reinforce shoulders, can form bands down the fronts of jackets to reinforce torn buttonholes, can extend fabric belts and can hold the ends of all sorts of mechanical closings, such as buckles. (Fig. 14.) You will come across the mention of leather as a means of mending again in this book. Keep it in mind whenever you face a difficult problem in mending outside garments, for there are many uses for leather in patching.

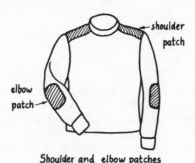

Shoulder and elbow patches

14

If you sew leather on your sewing machine, remember to use a large, strong needle. Leather can be "glued" to a material with liquid plastic adhesive.

Finally, you can always take your leather stitching problem to a cobbler.

Leather patches can be purchased as such, but it has been suggested that if not too large patches are needed, they can sometimes be cut from old leather gloves.

Patches that actually cover mends but are designed to appear as ornaments or as parts of the garment will be taken up in later parts of this book.

The Inset Patch This patch is neither placed under the material to be mended nor applied on the surface but is set into it. It is especially useful when there is a pattern that can be matched or a design that can distract attention from the seaming, if the garment is worth this rather fussy mend. (Fig. 15a.)

a. hole in figured or plaid material

15

Secure a piece of material exactly matching the material to be mended. (If you can't, employ some other means of hiding that mend.) A favorite source of patch material for this is a pocket that can be removed, but a thorough search of the inside of the garment may turn up a wide facing or some other bit somewhere that can be spared.

The hole is then usually made into a rectangle, since the seaming will be less noticeable if done along the "straight," or weave, of the material. (Fig. 15b.) Some adaptations can be made; suppose an

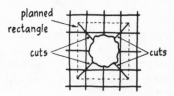

b. hole enlarged to planned rectangle

L-shaped tear is to be mended and the best available patch material is a long strip from somewhere inside. Then the strip would be cut and seamed at the corner of the L.

Turn under and baste back the edges of the tear to a depth of about a quarter of an inch, clipping the corners back just a little also, to allow the turning under. (Fig. 15c.) Lay the opened tear on the patch

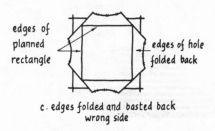

c. edges folded and basted back
wrong side

and match the patterns exactly. (Fig. 15d.) Stripes

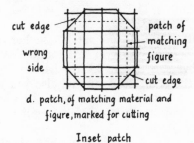

d. patch, of matching material and
figure, marked for cutting

Inset patch

in the material must join identical stripes in the patch, and designs in the material must continue precisely onto the patch. On the patch, as the material lies on it, mark by pins or basting threads the line where the hemmed-under edges of the material are to be turned back.

Now remove the material and take up the patch. Plan to turn under the hem about a third of an inch, so cut the edges of the patch back to this distance from the places you just pinned or basted. Cut away a little from each corner, to reduce bulk there when you turn the hem under. Then turn the edges under, on these pinned or basted lines, and baste down your one-third-inch hem. (Fig. 15e.)

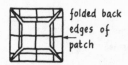

folded back
edges of
patch

e. patch, cut edges folded and
basted back
wrong side

Next, put material and patch together, matching stripes or designs, turn material and patch to the back and oversew the matched edges together. Turn to look at the front occasionally, else you may have to take out a line of stitching now and then and do it over, so that the patterns fit together perfectly. (Figs. 15f, g.)

Finally, press it all carefully on the right side.

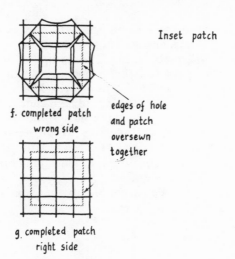

Inset patch

f. completed patch
wrong side

edges of hole
and patch
oversewn
together

g. completed patch
right side

DARNED MENDS._____

Darning is used instead of patching: first, for an unpretentious mend, in places where appearance is not considered to be important, as on underwear or towels or blankets; second, in sharp contrast, when appearance is very important indeed. It is used to mend worn or torn places on garments, such as skirts or coats, where a patch would have no chance to appear as other than a conspicuous mend, but where skillful darning might be able to produce a mend that would be much less noticeable or even difficult to find.

Just Darns Take up the first type of darning. To darn loosely woven fabrics in places that don't show, you use darning cotton, a soft multi-filament thread that fills the area better than sewing thread. If you have left-over bits of embroidery cotton, you may prefer to use them up instead.

Before the days of nylon hose, the feet of cotton and silk stockings always had to be mended, the heels especially. The problem might come up for you, and since the method is a basic one, with which you should be acquainted, it will be described here.

To begin, open out the place to be mended; stretch it, if necessary, to get it quite flat. To do this, your grandmother had, in addition to an embroidery frame, the "darning egg" (Fig. 16a), the "darning mushroom" (Fig. 16b), and the "glove finger darner" (Fig. 16c). You do not need them all; you can secure, today, a darning egg with a handle that is shaped to serve as a glove finger darner.

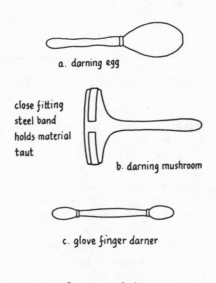

a. darning egg

close fitting
steel band
holds material
taut

b. darning mushroom

c. glove finger darner

Darning gadgets

16

You do not always darn from the right side of the fabric. The feet of your socks, for instance, do not show, unless you are addicted to wearing sandals, and you may feel more comfortable if they are darned from the wrong side. This is also true of darns, as well as other mends, in baby underclothing.

Having stretched the area to be darned over something, perhaps over your fingers, you observe the place where the darning is to take place. Don't be in a hurry to cut away any edges; often you can usefully incorporate edges into the darn.

When mending places that do not show, as the feet of socks, merely run your darning cotton from one side to the other, just catching it in the edges and pulling the edges rather loosely together. Then catch the upper edges to the lower, more or less, interweaving them with the crosswise stitches just made. Last, "fill in," and strengthen them with stitches more closely spaced, to really hold the darned stitches firmly in place.

Finally, extend the darning, carrying the stitches out beyond the actual hole, with multi-filament nylon thread. This will greatly strengthen the mend and, if you ever have to remend the place, will form a foundation on which to work.

If a towel is torn from the edge inward (Fig. 17a),

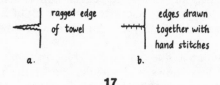

ragged edge
of towel

edges drawn
together with
hand stitches

a.   b.

17

catch the edges back together with a few hand stitches (Fig. 17b) and then unite the edges more

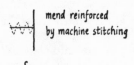

mend reinforced
by machine stitching

c.

Towel edge repair

firmly with back-and-forth machine stitching (Fig. 17c). But, to mend the worn edge of the bottom, turn a small hem and machine stitch it.

Holes in especially thick materials are dealt with in the section "Blankets."

Darning for Show   When a glove seam gives way, as they too frequently do, examine the seams and try to duplicate their appearance when making the repair. If they are hand stitched, this can be easily done. If they are machine stitched, the effect can be copied by repeated oversewing by hand, or sometimes by using one of the edge stitches used to hold the edges of buttonholes.

A hole not over a quarter of an inch in diameter, in thick, rough-finished material, perhaps a skirt, can be mended so it hardly shows by threading fine stitches through its substance without reaching the surface of the material, to draw the edges just together. The center is then cemented to a small patch underneath by a bit of fabric cement. This eliminates the necessity of turning the edges under; sometimes you may not wish to sacrifice even the bit of hem you would turn under if you were to sew it down to a patch.

For an area that has worn thin, in a place that more or less shows, the mender works the parts of the worn place back into their original positions and relationships to each other. If the area is very thin indeed or if stitches of the material are broken, a patch of matching color should be basted underneath and the material darned to it. This strengthens the mend and it also makes it less likely that the mended place will become puckered. You should keep in mind the tendency to pucker and not draw the thread at all tight as you work. In fact, it is advantageous to leave an extra bit of thread at the end of each line of darning.

As you darn, you should poke the raw ends of broken threads under and catch them down. In this, as in all darning, you should keep stitches that come to the surface, if at all possible, so short as to be nearly invisible. They can be longer on the wrong side.

Use a single-filament nylon thread for this, transparent for light-colored materials, dark for dark fabrics. The thin, stiff thread is a little difficult to manage at first, but here, as when used for machine stitching, it can be nearly invisible. You can also use human hair.

When the darn is finished, press the place, on the right side, under a damp cloth.

Woven-in Mending In rough-finished, not too tightly woven material, small holes and tears can be repaired with woven-in mending. This takes time and care, not to say contriving, but can be wonderfully helpful.

A small hole, not over a third of an inch in diameter, can be covered with woven-in threads of self material, drawn or raveled from inside seams, facings, etc. The weaving takes time, for withdrawn threads are short and they break easily. A darning needle is usually advised for this, but a shorter needle with a large eye, called a "tapestry needle," or a "chenille needle," is preferable, as these threads are more easily inserted into the extra-large eye and the short lengths of thread can be used up more com-

Tapestry needle

18

pletely with a short needle. (Fig. 18.) You will find a needle threader useful to get the thread into the needle.

Catch the end of the thread by a tiny stitch on the back of the material about a third of an inch from the hole (Fig. 19a), then bring the thread up through a matching stitch not more than a quarter of an inch from the hole. Carry it across the hole and insert it through the corresponding garment thread on the other side. Bring it back through another stitch on the same side of the hole and again carry it across. Continue this until the hole is covered.

But now you have only a set of parallel stitches across the hole. (Fig. 19b.) Start a set of stitches at right angles to these. (Fig. 19c.) If your first stitches went across, these go up and down. Where they cross the first set of stitches, they are to be painstakingly interwoven. If there is a pattern in the material, you should carry out the pattern, matching every stitch.

A Damask Darn If you want to mend a larger hole, perhaps a tear, study the material and consider its possibilities before you arrive at a solution to your problem. The older sewing books contain directions for mending holes, perhaps burns, in heavy linen damask. They describe setting into the hole a bit of the damask, cut exactly to fit, then holding it by fine darns over the edges. This might be worth trying on your thick wool garments, darning in the patch with withdrawn threads.

hole

a.

hole covered with
self-material threads,
one way only

b.

hole covered with
self-material threads,
both side to side and
up and down

c.

Woven mend

19

An Invisible Mend An English book gives directions for a combined patch-darn that is said to produce a completely invisible mend. First, secure a piece of material exactly matching the garment material and at least an inch and a half larger than the hole. Ravel the edges of the patch back to about a third of an inch from the hole edges. Then lay the patch on the hole and draw each thread, separately, through the fabric of the garment. These short threads are best pulled through from underneath, one by one, with a fine crochet hook.

This works beautifully, and is not too time-consuming, either, when worked on plain, unpatterned material. However, where there is any pattern at all to match, it is very difficult to get the matching stitches, everywhere, just where they belong. In patterned material, place a few key stitches, with a tapestry needle to anchor them just exactly where they belong in the pattern.

REPAIRING SEAMS _ _ _ _ _ _ _ _ _ _ _ _ _ _

A good understanding of seam repairing is worthwhile; a repaired seam can often be contrived not to show its mend very plainly. A useful or expensive garment can sometimes be rescued by an expertly mended seam.

A Pulled Seam A loosely woven material may pull away from a seam on one or both sides of the seam but the threads not break. (Fig. 20a.) Snip the *seam* stitches, being careful not to cut the material itself. Pin or baste a thin matching material under the pulled place. (Fig. 20b.) Catch the pulled threads down to the patch and then, either with thread that matches the material or, perhaps preferably, with transparent or dark nylon thread, sew back and forth, up and down and sidewise across the pulled threads, using a fine stitch (Figs. 20c, d), going no further than you must into the unpulled material. Use reverse stitching or machine darning.

Press. Stitch the seam (Fig. 20e) and press the seam open. If you are still not sure whether or not the seam will hold, stitch the seam on the surface, using, if you have it, the zigzagger. If you do not have the zigzag mechanism, stitch across the seam,

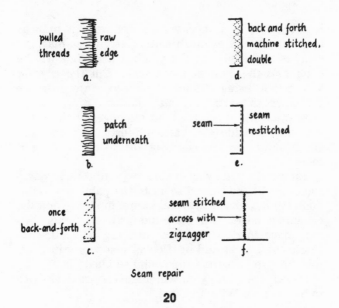

a. pulled threads / raw edge

b. patch underneath

c. once back-and-forth

d. back and forth machine stitched, double

e. seam → seam restitched

f. seam stitched across with → zigzagger

Seam repair

20

back and forth, with short reverse stitching or with machine darning stitches. (Fig. 20f.)

Frayed Edges Where the garment has pulled loose from a seam and the edges are worn, torn or frayed, patching is a necessity. Snip the seam stitches back to where the stitching was on firm material and put patches of strong cloth underneath the frayed area or areas. The patches may be held either by back-and-forth stitching or by being cemented to the material. Then restitch on the line of the original seam. Reinforce, as above, if advisable.

Washable materials are better stitched than cemented. Pin or baste the patch in place. Push and poke all those loose threads underneath and hem down the garment edge to the patch. Take it to the sewing machine and stitch back and forth, using short stitches rather closely spaced. (If this material is certain to be ironed with a hot iron, it may be better not to use nylon thread.) Carry these machine stitches to the edge of the patch, where they will be caught in the final garment seam. Cut the edge of your patch, using pinking shears, to conform to the line where the seam edge of the material ran.

Restitch the seam, then cut the edges of the patch one inch outside the back-and-forth stitching and catch down the raw edges of the patch to the garment.

Sometimes it may even seem wise to cement down the edges of the ragged seam to the patch and, after allowing it to dry for several hours, to strengthen the cemented edge with back-and-forth stitching. You may have to do this when mending a plastic-and-fabric coat. As is said in "Coats," heavy or stiff coats may have to have the seams hand stitched.

Pulled seams in nylon windbreakers are dealt with in the section "Windbreakers."

3

SPECIFIC PLACES
AND PROBLEMS

CUFFS_____

Cuffs offer a double problem: first, cuffs are conspicuous, and any mending at all should be completely disguised; second, cuffs get hard use, hence are often the first part of the garment (which might be an expensive coat) to show wear.

If it can be beautifully mended, that good coat, blouse or whatever can be worn a while longer, and often quite a while longer. However, a frayed shirt cuff often means a worn-out garment, so do not commence mending until you are sure it is worthwhile.

Cuff Edge Folded Under   When the cuff edge of a boy's knit cotton shirt is worn through, you can simply turn the frayed edge to the underside without even sewing on a binding and hold the frayed edge there with a row of machine stitching. The material must be stretched as one stitches or the child may not be able to get his hand through again.

In a coat of firm, closely woven material, the cuff edge may wear through with little actual fraying. (Fig. 21a.) The owner thinks of turning the worn edge under but fears to shorten the sleeve markedly. It may be possible to mend this cuff by turning under a tiny hem, not over a quarter of an inch deep, and holding it with a line of almost invisible hand stitches.

First, snip the lining loose, bring down the inside of the cuff and press the cuff edge flat. (Fig. 21b.) Then turn a new edge on a line just above the worn edge (perhaps a quarter of an inch above) and baste this in place. (Fig. 21c.) Then run a thread of match-

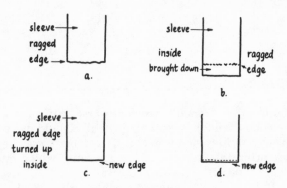

Frayed cuff folded inside

21

ing or slightly darker silk or of transparent nylon about the cuff, in that tiny hem, taking fine, close stitches that hardly show at all on the right side. This stitching must not be so "tight" as to dimple the outside surface of the cuff. When you come to one of the actual breaks in the material, catch the broken edges together with fine stitches. (Fig. 21d.)

The lining, shortened about a quarter of an inch, is then brought down and hemmed to, or over, the hand stitching.

This solution of the problem of reforming a worn cuff at the edge can be important; it once gave me greatly lengthened wear of a beautifully fitted made-to-measure winter coat.

Cuff Edge Turned Under and Covered by a Strip of Cloth The turned-under frayed edge (Fig. 22a) can be machine stitched to a strip of cloth the color of the material or of the lining. First, clip the lining loose, then bring down the inside of the cuff and press the whole cuff out flat. (Fig. 22b.) Next, carefully baste and stitch a wide covering strip to the cuff a quarter of an inch or so, on the outer side, above the ragged edge, right sides together. (Fig. 22c.) Turn the strip and the cuff inside, and baste so that the stitched edge of this new covering comes just under the edge of the cuff—just inside. Then bring the original sleeve lining down over the upper edge of the new covering. (Fig. 22d.)

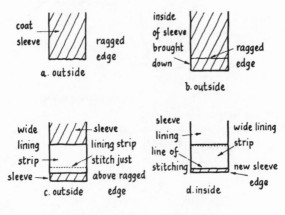

Frayed cuff brought down and covered by lining strip

22

Both Edges of Double Cuff Turned to Inside When the edge of a double cuff is worn through, turn the sleeves inside out and very carefully snip that inside, upper edge of the doubled cuff from the sleeve, right at the seam that holds the cuff to the sleeve. (Fig. 23a.) Then turn the cuff inside out, the inside up over the outside, and stitch around just above the worn or frayed edge. (Fig. 23b.) Finally, turn the cuff again, bring the edge you snipped back to the sleeve seam and hem or at least catch the edge to the sleeve seam. (Fig. 23c.) Machine stitch

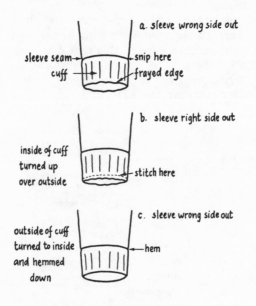

a. sleeve wrong side out

sleeve seam → ← snip here
cuff → frayed edge

b. sleeve right side out

inside of cuff
turned up
over outside
← stitch here

c. sleeve wrong side out

outside of cuff
turned to inside
and hemmed
down
← hem

Ragged edge of cuff turned to inside

23

around to hold it in place. It may be better to stitch around twice, to hold it more firmly.

If it is a good coat you are mending, snip the cuff lining loose (Fig. 23a), then turn the inside of the cuff over the outside, right sides together, and stitch around the cuff perhaps a quarter of an inch above the worn or frayed edge. (Fig. 23b.) Then turn the inside of the cuff back *to* the inside, press the new edge very carefully and replace the lining. (Fig. 23c.)

New Cuff from Sleeve Extension Once a man's jacket of red wool plaid was handed to the mending committee and was found to be in good condition except for frayed sleeve edges. (Fig. 24a.) (He must have had a job that was hard on cuffs.)

This was a coat where more than the usual material had been turned underneath at the cuff edge of the sleeve.

To mend it, the inside material was turned up over the outside and stitched around just above the frayed edge, as usual. (Fig. 24b.) But this time the stitched frayed edges were not turned underneath. They were left in place on the outside of the sleeve for a new cuff, and, instead, only the edge of the former inside material was turned down over it and tucked inside. The rest of the former inside was left out there for a new cuff. (Fig. 24c.) Only the lowest bit was turned back to the inside and covered by an extension of the sleeve lining. (Actually, an extension had to be put on the lining, to get it down where it could be hemmed to the inside of the new cuff.)

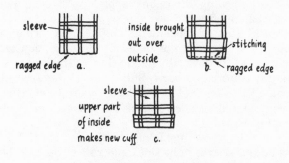

Cuff made from sleeve extension

24

Replacing Cuffs The knit cuffs of windbreaker-type coats, those cuffs, usually double, that keep cold air from going up the arm, are not as hard to replace as would at first appear, though the replacement does take some time and effort.

First, secure the replacement cuffs. Of course, you can knit them yourself. However, such cuffs, knit in the familiar knit-two-purl-two pattern, seem to lose their elasticity, their tightness, with wear. It must, nevertheless, be considered a good method for securing the needed cuffs in the right color and size.

You can buy the cuffs for fifty to seventy cents, which puts them out of the question for welfare sewing. Excellent substitutes, almost as good as the purchased cuffs, are the tightly knit ribbed tops of men's socks. And at times, lacking even that and trying desperately to find knit material in a color matching the coat, you might cut out cuffs from the bodies of discarded closely knit sweaters. If you try this, take the measurements (remember, the cuffs will be doubled), cut them out and stitch the lengthwise seams.

The following directions apply to all such cuff-replacement efforts.

Mark your replacement cuffs, from whatever source, at each of the doubled edges, in quarters. (Fig. 25a.) It is worthwhile to do this in thread of a sharply contrasting color. Snip the old cuffs from the coat. (Fig. 25b.) (I use a razor blade to cut these deeply placed stitches.) Mark the garment edge also in quarters.

Turn the sleeve inside out. Place the new cuff just inside the sleeve, right sides and raw edges together, matching the inside seams. Securely pin seams and quarter marks together. Baste or overcast the edges together, one thickness of the cuff to the full thickness of the garment-plus-lining; take to the machine and stitch. Turn a narrow hem in the other edge of the new cuff, pin it over the inside of the recent stitching, again matching seam and quarter marks, and hem it down by hand.

If you happen to use only a single thickness of

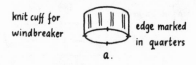

knit cuff for windbreaker — edge marked in quarters

a.

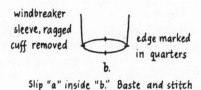

windbreaker sleeve, ragged cuff removed — edge marked in quarters

b.

Slip "a" inside "b." Baste and stitch

Replacing windbreaker cuff

25

new cuff, stitch it only to the outside fabric and hem the lining down over it. Of course, this procedure can be followed, if you prefer, with double-thickness cuffs, stitching the doubled edges only to the outside material of the sleeve and hemming the lining down over it.

It is a rather clumsy job to work at but one that a reasonably adept and resourceful person can do. The end result usually looks good and feels good to the wearer.

If after you get them on you find they are not close-fitting, put in an elastic that will hold the cuff closer about the wrist. To do this, run a line of stitching, by hand or machine, about an inch from the edge of the cuff and insert the elastic in this casing. You can also thread the fine elastic that can now be purchased in and out the material near the edge of the cuff.

Turning a collar   snip here

26

COLLARS_____

Turning the collar of a man's shirt is not difficult and is well worth while if you can catch it before the collar is worn through. Just snip the collar from the collar band (Fig. 26), turn the collar around and pin or baste it to the inside of the collar band.

Stitch them together, both thicknesses of the collar and the inside of the collar band. Try to make your line of stitching follow as exactly as possible the original line of stitching here.

Then tuck the raw edge of this seam you just stitched inside the collar band. On the outside of the shirt, bring the outer thickness of the collar band back up over your just-stitched seam. Either hem it back in place or baste or pin it in place and machine stitch it.

If you need to, you can purchase collar bands, in different sizes, and even new white collars.

SLEEVES_____

Frayed Elbow On a somewhat worn boy's or man's washable shirt, a frayed sleeve elbow is usually best taken care of by cutting across the sleeve at the top of the hole and hemming the upper part, making a short-sleeved shirt of it.

The next best mending is a cemented-on patch. Put a rolled-up newspaper inside the sleeve so the front does not get cemented to the back. If matching patches are carefully put on each sleeve, the beholder may be encouraged to think the manufacturer constructed it that way.

If you plan a careful, large, hemmed-in-place patch, consider snipping the sleeve seam and putting the patch in by machine stitching.

Tear at Wrist Placket When the placket at the wrist has given way and there is a little tear up the sleeve, if the garment is fairly good otherwise and if you can match the material well, a small patch underneath is not very noticeable. Start, always, by snipping the seam of the placket strip into which the sleeve was stitched. (Fig. 27a.) Insert your patch underneath the tear and pin it in place. Cut into the lower edge of the patch and insert the cut edge into the placket strip. (Fig. 27b.) Hem the edges of the tear to the patch and sew the cut edges into the placket. Catch down the edges of the patch underneath. (Fig. 27c.)

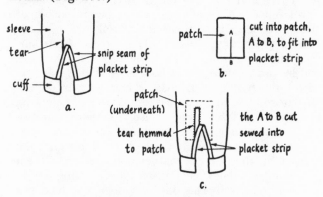

Mending tear into sleeve placket

27

Finally, reinforce the entire area by back-and-forth stitches or machine darning across the hemmed edges and across the placket-strip edges.

POCKETS_____

Pockets are frequent sources of trouble. They catch and pull and at their top corners they tear miserable little rents in the underneath fabric. Men carry little tools in their pockets and wear holes in them.

The Garment Around the Pocket When the garment is injured under or around a patch pocket, carefully remove the entire pocket and mend the tear as unobtrusively as possible, always reinforcing with a patch underneath. This may mean hemming the garment fabric to the patch or cementing the garment material down with fabric cement. Sew the pocket back, changing its location slightly so as to just cover and hide the mend. If this does not look right, replace it with a somewhat larger pocket of either matching or contrasting material.

If at the ends of inset pockets, on the front surface, the material is torn or pulled so that the mend will be conspicuous, cover both ends of both pockets with little triangular patches, of matching or at least harmonizing leather or cloth, carefully cementing them on with fabric cement. To give them a professional appearance, mark the outlines of the small triangular bits (not over three-quarters of an inch across) on the cloth or leather before you cut them out and sew about, just inside your cutting mark, using a fine stitch. The aim, of course, is to have the patches appear stitched on.

Repairing a Patch Pocket When a patch pocket itself needs mending, remove it carefully and study its possibilities. A strip of contrasting material or a patterned woven tape might be stitched across it to cover a hole. If the injury is near the lower edge, turn it wrong side up and face the new top. Of course, you can always replace it, but if it is a dress shirt, one prefers to have a pocket of self material. If you have to replace it, you might like to ornament the new pocket by putting a strip of material from the old pocket across it.

The Lining A worn-out pocket lining deserves some thought. Apparently everyone likes their pockets, so if the coat or pants is worth it, try to mend or replace the ragged pocket lining. It doesn't show, so the problem is simply to get it firmly mended without undue fussing. An ironed-on or cemented-on patch may do the trick (put a paper pad underneath). A corner hole can be simply stitched across, making the pocket a little smaller. If the lower end of the pocket is pretty well shot (Fig. 28a), snip the stitching where the two sides of the pocket are sewed together, but not where they are attached to the main garment (Fig. 28b), replace the worn parts with equally strong material, using simple machine-made seams across the pocket, cut the new pocket to the shape and size of the original and stitch the outside seams about as they were in the original pocket. (Figs. 28c, d.)

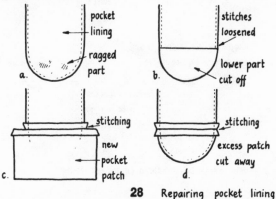

28 Repairing pocket lining

A worn-out pocket lining in a windbreaker—for instance, one of those zippered front pockets (Fig. 29a)—is not impossible to replace. Snip the worn lining loose (Fig. 29b), and cut a new pocket lining from two pieces of strong cloth. (If you can, match the color of the other pocket lining, for the lining color shows a little when the pocket is opened.) Stitch the two pieces of the new lining together, turn back the top edges of the windbreaker and baste in a half-inch hem. (Fig. 29c.) Pin the hem along the inside edge of the windbreaker where the original pocket stitching was snipped away and hand stitch the new pocket carefully and securely into place. (Fig. 29d.) Watch out that you do not take other parts of the windbreaker or the lining into your stitching.

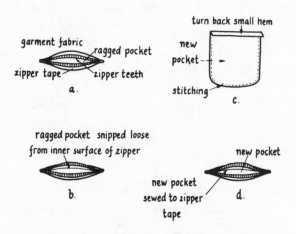

Replacing windbreaker pocket lining

29

THE CROTCH_____

Don't Narrow the Area When the seams in the crotch of the pants give way, there are quite a few raw edges of thick, sometimes wiry material to manipulate in a place that always seems awkward to work in. Keep in mind that none of the seams should be taken in any more than they were originally or movement will be hindered, the area will be under more strain than ever and will tend to give way again.

Method of Repair Remove the vestiges of broken stitches and snip open the seams back to firm material. You now have four separate pieces. Treat either the leg seams or the front-and-back sections separately at first; don't try to sew all four corners together at once.

If any edges are somewhat frayed, reinforce them with back-and-forth machine stitching, preferably using transparent or dark nylon thread. (Fig. 30a.)

If the edges of the material are badly frayed, patches are certainly called for. Use patching material that, though strong and firm, is not thick. This is no place to build up extra bulk.

Baste each quarter, along its edge, to its patch, catching down any loose edges and tucking under any loose ends of thread. Pin the outer edges of the patches back out of the way, where they will not get caught into the stitching. Stitch the frayed edges of the material to the edges of the patches with crisscross stitching. (Fig. 30b.) Cut the seam edges of the patches to correspond with the former seam edges of the material.

Then resew the seams, being careful not to take the

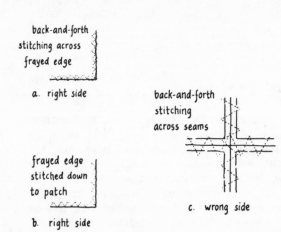

back-and-forth
stitching across
frayed edge

a. right side

back-and-forth
stitching
across seams

frayed edge
stitched down
to patch

c. wrong side

b. right side

Crotch repair

30

seams any deeper than they were originally, lest the general area be narrowed. Stitch the pant leg seams, then the front-back seams (or vice versa). Last, press open the seams, and, working from inside the garment, crisscross the seams with back-and-forth or machine darning stitching. (Fig. 30c.)

Inspect the area from the outside to make sure you have run the reinforcement across all the weak and worn places. Cut the outside edges of the patches neatly across, forming little triangles, and hold these outer edges in their places with herringbone stitching.

These methods of restoring ragged edges so that they can be restitched and become strong seams again should be kept in mind, for they are methods that can be used to repair and renew seams in other places.

THE UNDERARM._____

Where four seams come together under the arm, the process of repair is, of course, much like the repair of a crotch that has given way. There are some differences.

A repair here tends to show more than does a crotch repair. In all but smooth and shiny materials, however, one can stitch back and forth just across the seams, from the inside, and the stitches need not be too evident. Secure thread closely matching the material or, even better, use single-filament transparent or dark nylon thread (wound on the bobbin, if you stitch from the inside, for then the bobbin thread is the one that will show). The area is not quite as restricted a one to work in as is the crotch, and you do not usually have as heavy a material to work with.

You can reconstruct an underarm repair and have it appear better than might seem possible, in a coat where the original underarm stitching has torn loose. Cement the torn edges to a firm strong material that is very nearly the color of the coat fabric. Then, after the cement has dried for several hours, with back-and-forth stitching, sew the material edge to the patch. Next, cut the patch to the original line of the material edge and restitch the seam.

You will have to open the seam of the lining directly underneath the seam you are mending, to restitch the coat seam itself.

If you have done the work carefully, the mend need show very little.

LININGS_____

Constructing new linings to go into used coats is not an easy thing to do. If make one you must, the best thing to do is to look up a coat lining pattern the right size and use it, adapting it as well as you can.

You can also try taking a blouse of the right size, of good material, suitable color, and not much worn, turning it inside out and putting it in as a lining. Cut back collar and cuffs. If you are able to lay hands on the right blouse, this simple procedure could make possible a warm good coat for a child, without effort, time and cost out of proportion to the worth of the garment.

When a coat lining has worn out under the arms, it will rarely be possible to patch or darn the smooth material so it will look good. Instead, from material matching the lining, cut two pieces shaped like old-fashioned perspiration-proof dress shields, which are shaped like fat new moons. (Fig. 31.) Stitch the centers of the two pieces, right sides together; baste hems along the outsides and hem neatly into the armhole over the worn place. The idea is to give the impression that they are covered dress shields put in by the coat manufacturer.

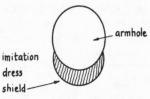

31   Mending ragged underarm lining

PLASTICS_____

Tears in plastics—for instance, in plastic raincoats —can be repaired so that the coat will still be serviceable, but the mend will show. With care, the mend can be made neat and unobtrusive, but on this shiny, smooth and more or less transparent substance, you cannot entirely hide the patches, unless they are in half-hidden places already, as under the arms.

Two methods are available for mending plastics: one, with ironed-on transparent, treated plastic patching tape, and, two, with a special liquid adhesive and a strong transparent patch.

If the directions are carefully followed, both methods work; the patches hold firmly. Obviously, the ironed-on patch would be the cheaper and preferable method if you have only one or two tears to mend. If you have a considerable amount of plastic mending to do and can find a sufficient amount of firm plastic to mend with, the liquid adhesive might be preferable.

Preparation With either method, the patch must be cut at each bend of the tear and a new length prepared to last until the next bend. The patch material does not stretch and should not be folded. (Fig. 32a.)

The manufacturers emphasize that the surface to be mended must be free from any trace of grease. They mean it! If you neglect this warning, the patch will not stick and can easily be peeled off. You can use a cleaning solvent, such as a dry-cleaning fluid,

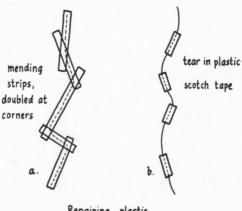

mending strips, doubled at corners

tear in plastic

scotch tape

a.

b.

Repairing plastic

32

or even soap and water, if the area is thoroughly rinsed and dried afterward.

It is difficult to keep the torn edges in exact contact while you apply the patches. Try holding them together with scotch tape. (Fig. 32b.)

Make each patch as efficient as possible. Press down all edges firmly. Cut all corners round, so there will be no sharp points to catch and pull the patch loose.

Perhaps the ironed-on patches better be put on the outside and the pasted-on patches on the inside, but it does not greatly matter.

Ironed-On Tapes First practice with ironed-on tape on a piece of plastic of a thickness resembling that of the plastic you are mending. Follow exactly the directions as to the degree and duration of the heat you apply. If you melt the patch into the pressing cloth, you must of course try a less-hot iron. If the heat is insufficient and the patch does not adhere firmly, repeat with an iron that is warmer.

The Pasted-On Patch   There is a length of patch material included with the tube of liquid adhesive you buy, and this is useful in itself, as well as showing the thickness that will always be needed in patching material with that liquid. Any plastic patch tends to crinkle and curl just a little when moistened with the adhesive. If you use any thinner material, it might crinkle and curl very badly. However, if for any reason you want to use thinner material, try this: apply the solution to a half inch or so of patch material and, without cutting it, stick the half inch down. Then apply the adhesive to the next half inch and stick it down, and so on.

But if you are following the standard directions, cover the under surface of the patch with the liquid adhesive, press it down well, being careful to press out any bubbles as completely as you can, and extend liquid and pressure out to the edges of the patch.

This liquid can also be used on fabrics and leather, but on fabrics, even thick fabrics, the liquid soaks through and shows as a dark line, and it does not hold too well. On leather it works better; here the surfaces must be held together with firm pressure for several hours.

4

FASTENINGS

BUTTONS
BUTTONHOLES
ZIPPERS

BUTTONS———————————————

A Missing Button   It is an unhappy incident when a button comes up missing from a matched series down the front of a coat or dress. If you possibly can, rematch or replace it, for one mismatched button can make a coat look second-hand and, sometimes, all but disreputable.

Examine the whole garment. There may be buttons on a partial belt at the back, or on a pocket. If the button had partly torn loose, it may have slipped inside the facing.

Ask your friends if they have a collection of discarded buttons you can look over for replacements. Older housewives are likely to have larger collections.

If adjust to the loss you must, change the buttons so that it is the lowest button that is missing. Often one leaves the lowest button unfastened and its loss is less noticeable.

If you buy replacements, consider the shiny metal ones. How they do dress up a humdrum dress. If you think your clothing is too dreary in color and effect, as any clothing may get to be, as it becomes old and faded, nothing helps cheer it up more quickly, in general, than gay, bright metal buttons. Use lots of them, if you can find places for them— say, on pockets and cuffs, on closings and belts.

Have you tried making homemade buttons? First, of course, there are the fabric-covered buttons, made either from wooden button molds or from buttons you may have that are the right size and shape. They need not be fabric-covered; you can make an especially fine-looking button by covering the button mold with soft leather, as from a left-over leather dress glove.

There are also those made from patented metal molds you buy, complete, on a card. An imported sweater I once owned had buttons made of the same yarn as the sweater. The foundation was a plastic ring and the yarn seemed to have been crocheted in from this plastic ring edge. On sports clothing, you may see buttons cut from very heavy leather. Also, there are buttons carved from fine-grained, often exotic, woods.

Sewing On the Button   When replacing a button, try to find thread matching that used to sew on the other buttons already in place.

Unless the button you are sewing on is purely for ornamentation, sew it on somewhat loosely. If sewed tightly, it is more difficult to fasten and may pucker both the upper and the lower fabrics. You can buy gadgets to hold the button up from the cloth as you sew it on, but this is not necessary. These contrivances can be easily fashioned from pieces of firm cardboard, from pieces of thick plastic, as the little catches used to hold plastic bags shut or from bits of flat thin wood, as popsicle sticks. Just cut a little slot, place the gadget on the cloth with the slot over the location of the button and sew the button in place through the slot. Last of all, wind the thread about your loose stitching two or three times, between button and material, and fasten it with a few tiny stitches, underneath where they do not show.

When sewing a large button to heavy material— say, a coat—consider sewing it through a small button, on the wrong side, underneath. This helps keep the large button from pulling the cloth away, under strain.

Have you considered fastening on buttons, especially coat buttons, with elastic cord? Buttons so fastened will button easily and, because they "give" to some extent when subjected to strain, tend to stay on longer than buttons fastened with unyielding thread. Unless the material is very loose in weave, do not try to draw the elastic cord through to the wrong side; sew it firmly to the outside of the cloth just under the button.

Frequently there is undue strain on the last button at the bottom of a dress that buttons all the way down the front. Try fastening this button on with elastic cord. You can also substitute a strong snap fastener here, and then sew the button on the outside, over the buttonhole.

Sometimes the stitching of a button partly tears the garment it has been sewed to (Fig. 33a.), the button may then slip inside the facing and appear lost, unless you know where to look for it. Take off the button and take out all the threads that formerly held it. If the garment was of thin material, slip a small patch inside the facing, under the hole. (Fig. 33b.) Catch down any loose threads (Fig. 33c) and reinforce with back-and-forth machine stitching (Fig. 33d), taking care not to run the stitches back

a. tear at site of button

b. site reinforced

c. edges caught (and some hemmed) down

d. area cross stitched

33

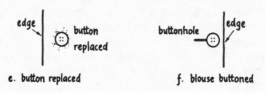

e. button replaced   f. blouse buttoned

Tear under button

very far from the edge, else they will show when the buttonhole side (the outside) is buttoned down. If carefully done, the stitching can usually be hidden when the garment is buttoned. (Figs. 33e, f.)

Prevention After you have settled many a problem with lost buttons, you may be able to summon the patience to do something you should have done long before—to examine every garment worn by anyone in your household, giving every button a little tug to make sure it is strongly sewed on, and resewing if it seems likely to come loose. You really should do this to any garment as soon as you buy it.

BUTTONHOLES _____

A frayed buttonhole (Fig. 34a) can be mended by hand or on the sewing machine.

You start by slipping a reinforcement between the thicknesses of the garment where the buttonhole is located. (Fig. 34b.) Non-woven interfacing is best for this, in my experience. With your needle, work the frayed edges, on the one side and on the other, into as nearly as possible their original positions and baste the material and the loose threads back where

a. ragged buttonhole

c. edges drawn firmly
together

b. reinforcement slipped
inside fold

d. buttonhole restitched

Buttonhole repaired by buttonholer

34

they belong. (Fig. 34c.) Use a fine matching thread or a single-filament nylon thread or human hair.

Even if you intend to hand stitch, or hand embroider, your buttonhole, when you are working in heavy, loose-woven material, as tweed, you may well prefer to machine stitch about the edges of the buttonhole first. Use a short stitch, of matching thread, and go around twice. (Fig. 34d.)

Hand Mending If you are mending this by hand, and if you have not stitched around the buttonhole by machine, run stitches by hand about the edges of the buttonhole, cut your buttonhole in the interfacing (the right length), overcast your stitches and go around the buttonhole—embroider around it, really —with one of the embroidery-style edge stitches. For this you will want to use the thick silk thread called "buttonhole twist," if you can get it in a matching shade. If you cannot, use a strong thread or a doubled thread.

There are two quite different embroidery stitches called "buttonhole stitch" by qualified experts.

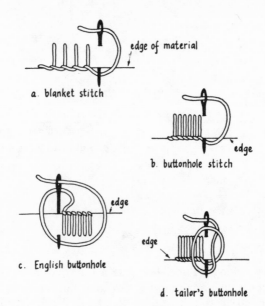

a. blanket stitch

b. buttonhole stitch

c. English buttonhole

d. tailor's buttonhole

Four edge stitches

35

One is the familiar "blanket stitch" (Fig. 35a), but when used as a buttonhole stitch, the stitches are worked close together. To form it, you insert the needle just above the edge of the buttonhole and bring the point out under the edge of the cloth, over the thread. (Fig. 35b.)

The other, also called "buttonhole stitch" by some writers in this country, is called a "twist" by English needleworkers. It is easily made, yet strong and neat-looking. To make it, bring the needle up through the cloth from underneath, as far from the edge as you want the width of the buttonhole to be. The thread is then passed under the point of the needle from right to left, and as the thread is pulled through, the knot is drawn back to the edge of the buttonhole. (Fig. 35c.)

The "tailor's buttonhole," another edge stitch, gives a lasting and good-looking buttonhole. For this, insert the needle just above the edge of the buttonhole, but when the point of the needle is brought out from under the edge, give the thread an extra turn about the needle, counterclockwise (left to right), and hold the little knot with your thumb as you pull it tight. Repeated, this will give a row of close little knots, forming a firm, strong buttonhole. (Fig. 35d.)

Machine Mending You can often produce the quickest and best-looking results by using your sewing machine buttonholer, especially if you have some expertise with it.

First, insert the interfacing between the layers of frayed cloth and baste the frayed buttonhole parts to it, carefully fitting the buttonhole edges into place on the front side and on the back side of the interfacing, with the inside edges of the buttonhole touching each other. You can carry your stitches across from side to side, as you will eventually be cutting open the inside of the buttonhole, of course. Use a wide stitch, or, better still, go around the edge twice, once with a narrow stitch and then with a wide stitch. Remember to use thread that matches the thread in the other buttonholes.

The same method can be used to mend an eyelet that has frayed, for there is a buttonhole template for eyelets.

What you must watch out for is keeping the machine exactly on the track of the old buttonhole or eyelet. The buttonholer itself feels no compulsion to do so and if not closely watched is more than willing to go marching off the track, outlining a new buttonhole beside the old one or off at an angle to it. Be sure you can see just where the old buttonhole was and be sure that is where your buttonholer is now stitching.

ZIPPERS ————————————————————

Prevention   If you are a person who is "always having trouble with zippers"—if, again and again, you rip the zipper that closes your skirt, perhaps taking a zipper tooth, or several zipper teeth, with it— hadn't you better break your habit of taking out your irritation or impatience on zippers? You can yank at a refractory button . . . and sew it back on. You can tear off a hook and eye, and inexpensively replace it. But don't take out irritation on a zipper unless you are prepared for an inconvenience quite out of proportion to what satisfaction you may have obtained. All the help it gave you is that now you have something different to be mad about. Is it worth it?

With jacket zippers especially, train your children to handle them gently, never jerking the slides. Zippers just will not stand rough usage. Keep the zipper "oiled" by rubbing beeswax or paraffin, perhaps from a small candle, along the edge of the teeth.

What is said in this section about repairing zippers applies almost exclusively to the metal ones. Any repairing of nylon zippers, beyond replacing slides, is extremely difficult. The only thing to be said for them is that they are easy to stitch over.

More experimentation is needed with various zipper replacements, such as replacing missing zipper teeth and trying to mend or replace the parts of the come-apart fastener of a separating zipper.

Tools and Parts Zipper mending is a specialty in itself. The worker can do simple stitching on zippers, but for actual zipper repair one needs to be somewhat mechanically minded and be able to use certain hardware appliances.

For good zipper mending, some extra tools are needed. There is no better tool than a large safety pin to poke zipper edges back into slides. A dull kitchen knife (a dull old paring knife that once had a point) pries up prongs. When you have a really complicated zipper problem, you also need small pointed pliers and a small pointed wire cutter. (Figs. 36a, b.)

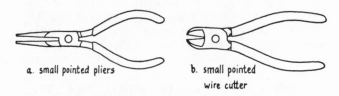

a. small pointed pliers   b. small pointed wire cutter

Pliers and wire cutter

36

Many housewives have a supply of used zippers they have saved. In the future, you would do well to keep even broken zipper parts as well as the whole ones.

The Pull Is Off the Slide The commonest problem seems to be that the little pull on the slide has come off. If there is a hole where the pull was attached, you can usually insert either a paper clip or a tiny safety pin as a pull. Some of the tiny safety pins have no loop at the end and are especially good for this. If there is no hole and no way of boring one, try to pry loose a pull from an old slide and work it on with the pliers.

The Slide Is Off One Side of the Zipper When the whole slide has come off one side of the zipper, examine the whole zipper before you put any work into it. Often a "tooth" is gone somewhere. (That is where the slide slipped off.) Can the zipper work acceptably even with a tooth missing? If the tooth is missing near one end, sew that place to the garment, and the slide thereafter can only go that far. If a tooth is missing midway, a careful person can still use the slide over the area. Will this zipper be used by a careful person? If it is a child's garment, and worth the time and effort, it will probably be better to put a new—or at least a complete—zipper on that side. (It is an amusing solution you may not have thought of to replace only half a zipper when only half is missing. When you can select from a collection of used zippers, as we on the mending committee could do, this short cut can be frequently resorted to.)

The Slide Is Off Both Sides of the Zipper When both halves of the zipper have come out of the slide and must be replaced, the slide is entirely loose from the garment, and you must see that it is put on right side up and right side out. Be sure the little pull is on the outside of the garment as you work on it. Unfortunately, it is easier to work if the slide is on the side on which you are working; you can hold and manipulate the slide by the pull. Unfortunately, also, you nearly always work from the inside of the garment. Even after long practice, you may still occasionally find you have carefully put a slide on wrong side to; the wearer would have to reach down inside the garment to pull it shut and he probably wouldn't be willing to do so. Therefore, if your slide is going into place too easily, be suspicious and see if you aren't holding the slide wrong side to.

Replacing the Slide To replace the slide that has

come off one or both sides of the zipper, open up the lower end of the zipper so you can get at the zipper ends. The lower ends of the ordinary "closed," or dress, zippers are held firmly together by small metal clasps with tiny prongs tightly caught underneath. Pry up the prongs with the dull kitchen knife. It is not easy to do; those prongs were put in to stay and they are hard to distinguish from the zipper teeth they were put next to. Pry them out and discard the bit of metal.

Note that the strip of tape the zipper teeth are fastened to has a distinct heavy ridge at the teeth edge. It is the lower end of this zipper ridge that must be inserted back into the slide. Snip loose the stitching that holds the end of the zipper tape to the garment fabric. Even if the slide is only off one side of the zipper, you may have to snip both sides from the garment to get the slide down where you can work the end that has come off back into the slide.

There are three ways to get the zipper back into the slide:

First, with a big safety pin as a tool, try to poke and pry the ridge at the very end of the zipper into the larger open end of the slide. (Fig. 37.) Sometimes it goes in quite easily, but if the end of the zipper tape is frayed or limp, you may have a difficult time.

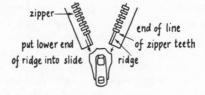

Replacing zipper teeth into slide

37

The second way is better. Sew a strong thread into the very end of the ridge that you want to get into the slide and pull the zipper through the slide instead of pushing it. Do not sew the end of the ridge into a thick club; take just a few stitches and try to use them to shape the end of the ridge to a little point. Use firm but not too thick thread for this task. Each zipper end, of course, must be stitched to a separate thread, for the slide has a bar dividing the larger open end into two distinct openings, one for each half of the zipper.

The third method is a short cut that can be used where there is room for some manipulation below the lowest teeth on the zipper. Be warned that you run some danger of breaking the slide apart when you use this method. If conditions are right, however, you may want to try it. Work the upper and lower halves of the slide apart, preferably with the pointed wire cutter. (Fig. 38a.) Make the opening just wide enough so that you can pull the ridge back into place between the upper and lower halves of the slide. (Fig. 38b.) For this, use that part of the ridge which is down below the lowest zipper tooth. Having replaced the zipper into the slide, finally, with your pliers, gently press the parts of the slide back together, with the upper and lower halves as far apart as they were originally. (Fig. 38c.)

When you get the slide entirely on the zipper, using any of the three methods, adjust the length of the ends so that the lowest zipper teeth are nearly opposite each other, and start working the slide up to them, locking the lowest zipper teeth together.

Now stop! As soon as a couple of interlocked teeth show below the slide, stop and sew the lower ends of the zipper together, right next to or over those lowest teeth, replacing the little metal clip you pried off. (Fig. 39.) This prompt stitching is necessary; un-

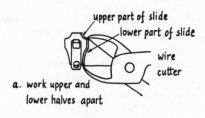

upper part of slide

lower part of slide

wire cutter

a. work upper and lower halves apart

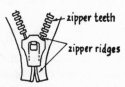

b. insert ridge of zipper teeth between halves of slide

zipper teeth

zipper ridges

c. pinch halves of slide back as they were originally

pliers

Opening slide to replace zipper

38

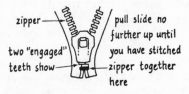

zipper

two "engaged" teeth show

pull slide no further up until you have stitched zipper together here

Stitch zipper together below slide

39

ZIPPERS   95

fastened zipper teeth below the slide will soon unlock. This would be a catastrophe, for relocking the loosened teeth below the slide is almost impossible. (Yet, to be completely truthful, it can sometimes be done. When only a few teeth have come apart, you may be able to interlock them again by an indescribable process of rubbing the teeth together, working them into place and pushing individual teeth with your thumbnail.)

Ordinarily, when the zipper has opened to any extent below the slide, to make it all workable again you need to take the slide off the top of the zipper and replace it from below. Even with thread sewn in, it is almost impossible to reinsert the closed zipper top into that small end of the slide. So don't forget to sew those lower ends together promptly. If you pulled the zipper back into the slide by the second method, you already have the threaded needle right at hand.

The Slide Is Lost   When the slide has been lost, you must find one that works and will fit. If you do not have any left-over zippers or zipper parts, ask your friends if they have any. Will it be worthwhile to *buy* a new zipper with a slide the right size? Possibly, if you can find a small (and therefore cheap) zipper the right size for your needs. Compare any in the store with your incomplete zipper and be sure it is the right size before you buy it and take it apart.

The Slide Is Rusted in Place   If the slide has rusted in place, the pull has usually been tugged off, too.

At the lower, narrower end of the slide, insert the point of your kitchen knife between the upper lip of the slide and the firmly closed zipper and work them apart, lifting the upper part of the slide. Then turn the whole zipper over and similarly work the lower lip of the slide from the lower surface of the zipper itself. The upper and lower lips of the slide can also be separated by using the wire cutter, as was mentioned when the third method of getting the slide back on the zipper was described. Having separated the upper and lower lips of the slide from the zipper, grasp the slide in your pliers and pull hard. You may need to clamp the other end of the zipper to something or have a friend pulling against you.

You can also put a drop of rust-eroding fluid into the slide, first snipping, for a couple of inches up and down, the stitching that holds the zipper tape to the garment, so that you can work on the frozen zipper with the fluid without fear of injury to the adjacent material. Also, put several thicknesses of paper under the zipper, between it and the material, as you work. If the first drops do not loosen the zipper, add another drop or two of the fluid and wait for it to work in.

When the whole zipper has been restored to normal working condition, rinse out any rust-eroding fluid you may have used, pinch the lips of the slide back into place with your pliers and rub plenty of paraffin into the zipper edges.

Slide Adjustments Another uncommon problem is that the upper and lower parts of the slide may have become too widely separated or, on the other hand, too closely clamped together. The possibility should be kept in mind when a problem that seemed simple proves unexpectedly difficult to solve. When a slide that has seemed in every way the right size slips on but will not lock the teeth together, examine it to see if the upper part of the slide is too far from the lower. If so, pinch them together with your pliers. Again, when you cannot force the zipper edge into a slide that seems a good fit, see if top and bottom are too narrowly closed together. If they are, work them apart with the kitchen knife or the wire-cutter.

• Replacing Zippers

Select a fairly strong metal zipper. Look over those available; you may prefer one that has colored teeth or teeth covered with cloth of the same color as your material. If you cannot find a zipper of just the right length, buy one a little too long rather than one too short. You can always sew the extra teeth together at the lower end and poke them out of sight.

Putting a Zipper into a Placket   The general procedure is to place the placket on the zipper. First, you sew the underlap to its side of the zipper, not far from the teeth. Finally, you bring the overlap over this, covering zipper, underlap and stitching, and carefully stitch the overlap to the other half of the zipper.

In a man's fly, the underlap is stitched to the right side of the zipper. In a woman's skirt, whether the closing is in front or on the left side, the underlapping and overlapping are the opposite of this.

Assume that you are to put in a fly zipper.

Start with the underlap. At this stage, it is more convenient to have the zipper closed. Lay the zipper under the underlap of the fly, the top exactly where you want it to be sewed in place, and pin it there. Poke the bit of extra tape at the top, beyond the zipper teeth, out of sight into the belt of the pants (probably there is just enough opening to receive it, since the old zipper was at one time sewed in there). Pin that in place.

Now pin the edge of the underlap of the fly, where it was formerly stitched to the old zipper, to the zipper tape about an eighth of an inch from the zipper teeth all the way down to the lower end of the zipper. Then baste it in place, top and entire length. (Fig. 40a).

You may or may not have an additional small strip of material, usually the same as your garment material, stitched underneath as an additional pro-

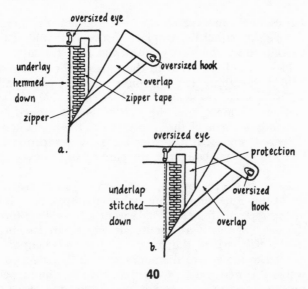

oversized eye

underlay
hemmed
down

oversized hook

overlap

zipper tape

zipper

a.

oversized eye

protection

underlap
stitched
down

oversized
hook

overlap

b.

40

tection. If so, now baste that in place also, just where
it was before, and sew it. (Fig. 40b.)

Does it look all right? Is it smooth and flat, the
upper end of that half of the zipper hidden?

If so, stitch it in place, starting at the very top. If
you are a novice-mender, it would probably be better
to do it by hand. Having secured the top neatly, next
stitch through the fold of the pants material and the
zipper tape and the underneath protection, if there is
one, about an eighth of an inch from the zipper
teeth. Better still, hem it down at the edge, then stitch
it by hand or on the machine, using the zipper presser
foot, back from the edge. The hem alone is not strong
enough to hold it for any length of time.

Fold the protecting band back and pin it out of the
way. Now close the zipper and lay the overlap of
the placket in place over the zipper and stitched-in-
place underlap. Be sure the two upper ends of the
zipper are equally far from the belt. Fasten the but-

ton or hook and eye of the belt, and smooth down the overlap so all lies in place just as it should. The overlap must completely cover and hide the zipper.

Now pin the overlap to the tape of the unsewed half of the zipper. Pin it in more than one place and adjust it so it lies smooth. Look at the inside of the garment to make sure the overlap is not pinned to the underlap side of the zipper, nor to the protection, if there is one. If it has come loose, the protection is likely to become caught in the pinning of the overlap of the placket.

Next, baste the overlap to the tape you pinned it to. At this time, find out just where the uppermost bit of the tape of this (left) side went out of sight into the belt (again, there should already be an opening in the belt, where the former zipper end went in) and baste the end of the new zipper in there. As you work, you may need to unzip and zip up the zipper repeatedly to make sure you are sewing the overlap to the tape and only to the tape and keeping it smooth and in place. Occasionally lay the zipper down and smooth the overlap out, to make sure it will be smooth and unpuckered when it is done.

When it is basted in place, sew it, from the underneath or zipper side, either by hand, using the backstitch, or on the machine, using the zipper presser foot. The overlap will lie flatter on the zipper if it is not stitched very near the teeth of the zipper. It is worth the effort to put it on by machine stitching if you can, for it will look better. Don't be afraid to take out your stitches and do it over if it does not look right.

Last, unfasten the protection and adjust it, flat, underneath. Fasten it to the belt. Then continue your backstitch or machine stitching across the bottom of the overlap, below the lower end of the zipper (if you have a too-long zipper, you will have to go stitch by

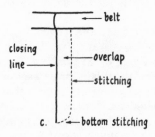

Replacing a zipper in a placket

stitch, not to break the sewing machine needle on the zipper), to about where the stitching of the underlap ended. (Fig. 40c.)

Dress Zipper Replacement First, there is what the zipper manufacturer calls a "lapped application." This has an overlap, like that of a placket, and you put in such a zipper in the same way described for those in placket openings.

Second, the mender may plan to have the two sides of the material meet over the center of the zipper all the way down.

For this, the directions that come on the card with the zipper usually direct you to loosely stitch the two sides of the garment together, then open the seam and press it flat. Sew the garment to the zipper tape on both sides of the teeth, and, finally, take out your loose stitches, leaving the two narrow overlaps separate but meeting in the middle of the zipper.

When replacing this zipper, baste (loosely overcast) your center edges together, then, carefully follow the manufacturer's directions for putting in new zippers. That is, on the wrong side, put the zipper in place wrong side up on top of the center basting you've just done and, using your zipper presser foot, stitch up the sides on the sewing machine.

Unless you baste those edges together first, the zipper will not look as if it had been expertly put in.

The Jacket-Type, or Separating, Zipper The last major problem in this zipper section concerns a jacket-type, or separating, zipper that has become inoperative while the general condition of the whole jacket is still good. If you want to tackle the problem of replacing that zipper yourself, you will need, in addition to a new separating zipper, some experience in sewing and a great deal of patience.

Let me emphasize that need for patience. If you are the type that soon loses your temper, pushes material and zipper hastily into some sort of order, pins it and more or less sews it into place, wrong place or right place, as long as the bothersome job gets done somehow—if you are that type, find someone else to put in the new zipper. Zipper replacement is a task for one who can be careful and patient. On the other hand, if you will use patience, which may even mean taking out some stitches and doing a part over, even if you are not an expert needleworker you probably can do it.

Begin, of course, by securing a replacement separating zipper, long enough, strong enough, and, if your coat is reversible, with a pull on both sides of the slide. If you must, you can use a zipper longer than the old one, folding the excess and tucking it in between the outside and the lining, at the top.

With a sharp edge, such as a razor blade, cut the old zipper from one side of the jacket front. Here is the place to start practicing care and patience. See every stitch before you cut it. A wrong stitch sewed can be replaced; a cut into the substance of the jacket, outside or lining, cannot, but must later be mended as best you can. Remove the old zipper from only one side, so you can consult the other side to see just where and how to put in the new zipper. To cut loose the top end of the zipper you may have to snip some deeply placed stitches that hold the folded-under end of the zipper to the jacket front and collar. Use care—again, see each stitch you cut.

Having removed the zipper from one side, pull out all the loose stitches. Are the two edges, jacket outside and jacket lining, flat and smooth and easy to work with? If either edge is wrinkled or crinkled, press it. If one surface is of artificial fiber, such as nylon, remember not to use too hot an iron.

Then baste this hem you have just ironed flat back to the width it was when it was stitched to the old zipper. Ordinarily, the edge of the jacket outside is stitched to the zipper with a fairly wide hem, so that the wide hems meet and more or less hide the zipper. The lining, on the inside, is sewed to the zipper tape with almost no hem.

In the directions that follow, the jacket outside is stitched first, then the lining is hemmed to the inside of the half zipper.

Be sure you have the zipper right side out, so the little pull on the slide is on the outside.

Pin half the zipper against the inside of the jacket exactly where the old zipper was stitched. (Figs. 41a, b.) Use plenty of pins, securely placed. The lower end of the zipper is usually placed where the end was before, but it can be higher or lower if you have a good reason for changing it. The tape has been reinforced at the lower end, and is thick and hard and not easy to sew through. Stitch it as strongly and as neatly as you can. (Fig. 41c.)

I advise sewing all in place by hand with a "back-stitch"—the long stitch on the inside of the zipper, the single small stitches on the outside surface. (Fig. 41d.) Use a strong thread. Consult the old

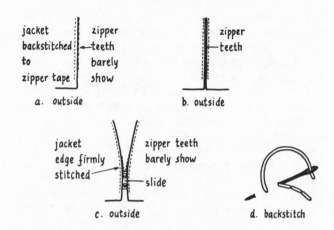

a. outside

b. outside

c. outside

d. backstitch

Replacing a separating zipper

41

zipper you left on the other side to ascertain where to sew. The outside stitching should be the same distance from the edge as before, and there should be the same width from the zipper teeth to the hemmed-down edge of the lining on the inside.

At the very top, fold any extra zipper inside the jacket, as I already advised, between outside and lining. Or, if you have pliers and a pointed wire cutter and some skill and practice, you can remove the extra teeth, save the wide tooth that kept the slide from coming off, and pinch this wide tooth in place again at the new top.

Do you wish to run a line of machine stitching over your backstitch? Unless you are quite skillful in the use of the zipper foot, I suggest you get someone who is an expert with the zipper foot to do it for you. It is not easy to guide the stitching just where you want it to go along such a thick pad of material. If you do it yourself, proceed slowly and carefully.

The lining should usually be hand hemmed against the back side of the zipper. (Figs. 42a, b, c.) You may have to adjust your method to different edges of different linings, as imitation lamb's wool lining with a nylon-covered cord at the zipper edge, for instance. Study the other side and copy it, being sure your stitching takes in and holds all the different parts, if there is more than one fabric to be hemmed down to the inside of the zipper.

The experienced mender may prefer to machine stitch both lining and outside to the zipper. If only one seam is to show on the outside, which is preferable, the lining should be stitched first. The machine stitching will then go right through the lining, the zipper and the jacket itself.

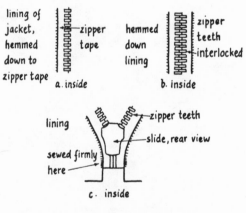

Replacing lining of separating zipper

42

So much for the complete replacement of the separating zipper. Often, the lowest inch or two of any separating zipper pulls loose from the garment. Take time to sew it back neatly and firmly, with thread matching the color of the garment or with transparent or dark nylon thread, and hem the lining back over it. (Figs. 43a, b, c.) It is a place that shows, and unworkmanlike mending is plainly evident.

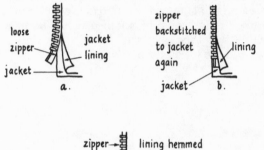

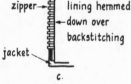

Repairing loosened lower end of separating zipper

43

5

THE GARMENTS

CHILDREN'S CLOTHING
BABY GARMENTS
UNDERCLOTHING
WORK CLOTHING
DRESSES
COATS
WINDBREAKERS

CHILDREN'S CLOTHING_____

"The mother, wi' her needle and her sheers,
Gars auld claes look amaist as weel's the new."

The mother in Burns's "The Cotter's Saturday Night" could make the auld claes look amaist as weel's the new the more readily because she was probably mending children's clothing; children's clothing has a less rigid styling and the mother's fancy can be freer.

Yet children's garments have plenty of problems of their own. Seams pull loose, bindings pull off and children tear and stain the fronts of their clothing more than do most adults.

Mend Them with Care   Stop and take time to put a pulled seam back together and stitch it carefully, for it can often be made to look "as good as new." If you can force yourself to do a workmanlike job the first time—putting the gathers back into the skirt evenly, basting, stitching, examining your work, re-stitching—careful mending can come to be a habit, with great resulting peace of mind, for a mother will have to look often at the garment she has mended, for good or ill.

Mend Them with Imagination   For the mending of small children's garments, use your imagination and get some fun out of it. Fancy patches, bright buttons, rickrack braid are yours to cover up with. You might even show your project to the child who is to wear the garment and get his or her reaction to your ideas (and later, with mixed feelings, hear your little girl, for instance, boasting to everyone, "See how my mommy fixed that place I tore in my dress.")

As has been said elsewhere, look for useful ideas. Visit stores where children's clothing, including imported clothing, is sold. Note how far prevailing styles sanction the use of front ornamentation. As you look, keep in mind any materials you may have that could be made use of for patch ornaments, buttons for trimming, etc. Remember that rickrack can be made to look like various objects. Save bits of rickrack when you discard aprons and housedresses.

• Cover-Ups

Sometimes for a small hole you may be able to spare a little of the garment material, perhaps from a facing somewhere inside, and use it, cut in some fancy shape, as a patch cover-up. Certain oddments of printed cloth, also, would be especially good as cover-ups; appliqués of conventionalized flowers or circus characters, for instance, could be cut out and stitched or cemented down over a front mend. Many other shapes can be improvised and used as appliquéd cover-ups. (Figs. 44a, b, c, d.)

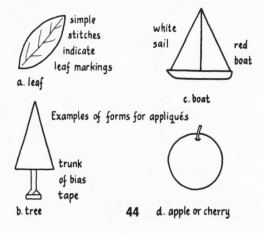

simple stitches indicate leaf markings

a. leaf

white sail   red boat

c. boat

Examples of forms for appliqués

trunk of bias tape

b. tree

44   d. apple or cherry

Constructing an Appliqué One good way to construct a simple appliqué is to baste the appliqué material to a pattern or "template" of stiff paper, as follows:

Having selected your design and drawn or copied it in exactly the size and shape you want to use, draw the design on stiff, strong paper. (Fig. 45a.) Cut it out and use it as a pattern from which to cut the appliqué, allowing a quarter to a third of an inch all around to turn under as a hem. (Fig 45b.)

Now baste the material to the paper template (Fig. 45c), turn the edges of the material under and baste them underneath, cutting away some excess at corners to avoid bunching there, and shaping the appliqué exactly as you want it to appear on the dress. (Figs. 45d, e.)

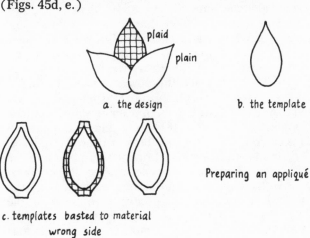

a. the design

b. the template

Preparing an appliqué

c. templates basted to material
wrong side

45   d. hems turned and basted

e. prepared appliqués
right side

f. completed
appliqué

Preparing an appliqué

Next, dampen and press it, to secure a firm, sharp edge around the appliqué. When this is done to your satisfaction, remove the stitches that basted it to the paper and the paper, and pin and baste your completed appliqué onto the dress. Hand hem it down with fine, careful stitches that show as little as possible. It is advisable to also machine stitch it, about its edges, to the dress, so that the appliqué will look as if it were part of the dress when you bought it. (Fig. 45f.) If you use cotton thread, loosen the thread tension; even if you preshrink the appliqué, the cotton thread will shrink, sometimes noticeably.

Pockets? Can you cover the mend with a pocket? This could be of either matching or contrasting color, and could well be balanced by another pocket on the other side. How about a pocket shaped like a flowerpot, with stem, leaf and flower appliquéd on the fabric just above it, apparently arising out of the flowerpot. A gingham dog and a calico cat? An imitation apron sewed right into the dress? There is even a "double pocket," a rectangle with the two upper corners cut out. Try it to cover a bad stain across the front of the garment. This double pocket is also known as a "kangaroo pocket"—a title whose aptness is quite apparent once the pocket is in place. (Fig. 46.)

• Little Boys' Pants

The mending of little boys' pants deserves special consideration, as do the little boys themselves. While the general problems are taken up in the section "Work Clothing," the worn-out knees of small boys' pants constitute a problem that is only too common. If this could be solved, it would be a great satisfaction to the boy, his family, and to all beholders.

The simplest solution is to cut a patch from firm, strong material, large enough to cover not only the hole but the worn area about it, and cement it on. You only need run the cement about the edges of the patch. For the tiny child tumbling about the sand pile, this should be sufficient.

A boy of school age or even kindergarten age does not like to wear obviously patched pants. Can the patch be disguised? Can you more or less fool the public about that patch? The impression you wish to produce is that the manufacturer planned and made the pants with the patch there and that the owner likes it that way. It follows that even if only one knee is worn out, the two knees must be patched alike.

There are boys' pants on which the manufacturer has sewed three varicolored patches diagonally down

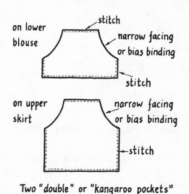

Two "double" or "kangaroo pockets"

46

across the knees, a lower corner of each overlapping by about a third the upper corner of the patch below. More common is a patch that might better be called a reinforcement, of closely matching material (this is most easily found when the pants are of the familiar blue denim) completely covering the full width of the knee section of the pants, stitched across the top and bottom and sewed firmly into the side seams.

These were stitched on. If you think stitched-on patches will be more acceptable to the owner of the pants than cemented-on ones, unless you have a free-arm sewing machine, snip the seams of the pant leg, flatten out the material and sew on your patch, then turn the pants inside out and restitch the seams. To give a professional appearance, any patches must be cut square or rectangular and placed exactly opposite each other.

Romper Suspenders When a small child breaks or loses one of his suspenders, you *can* purchase a replacement that has clasps holding it to the pants. Otherwise, make suspenders of a matching color and material. Cut them about two inches wide, turn in the raw edges and stitch together as if you were sewing the edges of a bias binding.

BABY GARMENTS._____

When you have the problem of mending a baby's clothing, you consider the baby's specific needs, often different from those of the older child and certainly from those of an adult.

Of course, the mother restitches seams, hems the edges of a hole to a patch and machine darns back and forth to reinforce it. She catches together the edges of a hole in knit underwear and takes a few back-and-forth stitches across it on her sewing machine.

But there are special problems that have to be considered when you're wondering whether to mend a baby's garment. If you live in a quite cold climate, for instance, you mend nearly every warm garment the baby has until he outgrows it, for you need extras to use if an outside garment, especially, gets wet, for thick clothing dries slowly in cold weather.

The Crotch Angle In these little garments the lower part often pulls away from the upper at the angle of the crotch. This is a point of considerable strain and it is advisable to mend it by putting in a patch. If you think there will still be too much of a strain on the area even when you have mended the existing hole, open the seams a little further in each direction, making an even larger hole. Put a patch of preshrunk, soft material underneath, hem the edges of the garment down to the patch and reinforce the hem with back-and-forth stitching. Cut back the edges of the patch to the edge of the machine stitching and overcast with a herringbone stitch.

Replacing Snaps The self-covered patented snaps that close the leg and crotch opening too frequently tear and burst loose. If this occurs in an undergarment, which is not exposed to public gaze, a couple of snap fasteners sewed on either side of the snap that gave way will take care of it. If it is in an outside garment and worth some care and attention, try this: with the pointed wire cutter described in "Zippers," you cut and pry off the parts of the affected snap, mend and reinforce the torn part, then replace the snap, using one of the self-covered button gadgets that can be bought at notion counters. If you are uncertain as to which will be the best and easiest to put on, talk it over with the clerk.

You can also buy a gadget to replace the snap itself, but these are far from inexpensive.

Right Side?   One is sometimes puzzled as to which is the right and which is the wrong side in baby garments, especially in their undergarments and night wear. No doubt the idea is that it is more important to have the more comfortable surface next to the baby, whether or not it is the more attractive surface to look at. The quickest way to ascertain the right side may be to look at the zipper. The zipper pull will reliably be on the right side.

• Foot Coverings

The mending of the worn feet of baby rompers and sleepers is one of the problems that only the mender of baby garments often meets. Characteristically, the problem is that the toes have worn through or there are worn places or even holes in the little soles.

Soles   You can usefully mend the holes in the soles with patches cemented on with fabric cement. (Put a fold of paper inside so the top of the inside does not get cemented to the sole.)

For more extensive mending, you will probably have to take the sole off the upper, at least in the area where the mending is required. Cut enough of the stitches that hold sole to upper so that you can easily get at all the area to be mended.

You may be able to reinforce the worn place in the sole with machine darning. (Fig. 47a.) If you need a patch or replacement for the sole, try to secure easy-to-dry material—cloth that is strong but not thick. Stitch the patch across the sole and carry your stitching out to the edge, basting it in place, cutting it to fit, and then basting or overcasting the edges of sole and patch together. Last, stitch sole and upper together over your basting or overcasting stitches.

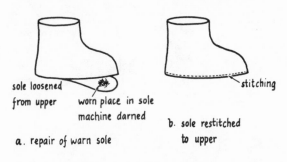

sole loosened from upper

worn place in sole machine darned

stitching

a. repair of warn sole

b. sole restitched to upper

Repair of sole of baby rompers

47

Stitch around twice—or use the zigzag stitch, if you have it. Remember to use a strong needle for this stitching. (Fig. 47b.)

This edge can well be finished by a line of button-hole stitch. You could also stitch a bias binding about the edge. This would look and wear well, but rompers and sleepers are garments that are washed often and the thick line of stitched fabrics would take time to dry.

If the soles are ragged, snip them off and use them as a pattern to cut out new soles from strong (and, if possible, from quick-drying) material. If you are unsure of the exact size to cut the new soles, be sure to make them large enough. The little feet can adjust to soles that are too floppy, but if you make the soles too small, it will be very hard on the baby.

Uppers To mend where the toes wore through the upper (Fig. 48a), make a patch from a fold of flan-nelette or cotton-knit material (that is, the new upper will be of double thickness) and sew it right over the instep of the old upper, from the middle of the sole edge on one side to the middle of the sole edge on the other. (Fig. 48b.) The material need not match in

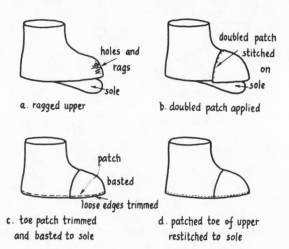

a. ragged upper

b. doubled patch applied

c. toe patch trimmed
and basted to sole

d. patched toe of upper
restitched to sole

Repair of baby romper toes

48

color or design; a bright figure or an amusing design
will do very well. Cut the patch edges to correspond
with the old seam line of the upper, then cut away
the old ragged material underneath and baste or
overcast the new line of the patch to the sole. (Fig.
48c.) Pin and baste the upper to the sole first, for
there will be some fullness to be taken care of. Then,
as before, stitch twice, or zigzag stitch, about the
edge over the basting or overcasting stitches. (Fig.
48d.)

UNDERCLOTHING_____

Repairing worn or torn underclothing presents a
somewhat different problem from the repairing of out-

side garments. Approach the problem of repairs in undergarments very critically. When a slip, for instance, starts to show wear, it is often, like the deacon's one-hoss shay, ready to fall to pieces all over.

When repairing underclothing, you can often find unexpected uses for elastic and also for fabric cement, if you keep their availability in mind. A connection pulls off or pulls apart, perhaps repeatedly. How about replacing it, or part of it, by a length of narrow elastic? A hose fastener of a child's garter is badly worn; a short strip of strong cloth cemented along its back can prolong its usefulness.

If you decide that a worn slip is worth some repairing, try at least to do most of the mending on the sewing machine. A seam that has come loose would be worth restitching, but knit material better have the edges overcast together first, for the edges curl up and are then hard to bring together evenly. Remember to stretch knit material as you stitch it.

Shoulder Straps If a shoulder strap has worn out, discard the little metal or plastic slides and put on straps the right length for you. Ribbon and tape are now expensive; you can easily stitch your own straps. Use fine material firm enough to hold a fold; cut it three-quarters of an inch wide, fold in the edges and stitch.

You will find it useful to replace the lowest two inches of each shoulder strap, in back, with quarter-inch-wide elastic. This "gives" comfortably with movement, and the straps will not pull loose or break as often as a strap that has no elastic in it would do.

If the straps have torn the edges of the slip where they were attached, try to make a neat, careful mend when reattaching them, selecting whatever method will add strength yet show the repairing as little as possible. If the tear is in lace, catch the edges together with a fine thread, then reinforce with machine darning and catch to the shoulder straps; however, make the main attachments of the straps down to the firmer garment material to which the lace itself is stitched.

If the top of the material has become torn where the straps were attached, as often happens, bring the torn edges together in little tucks and darts, then reinforce by a patch of thin but strong material underneath, hemmed to the material as inconspicuously as possible. Hand stitch the end of the shoulder strap underneath, making your stitches reinforce your patch if you can.

By the way, if your shoulder straps have an annoying habit of slipping down your arms, you can sew tapes, a bit over two inches long, to the inside of the shoulder seams of your dresses to hold the shoulder straps in place. Then sew a snap fastener on—one part to the shoulder seam near the collar, the other to the doubled upper end of the tape. (Fig. 49.)

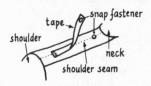

Shoulder-strap holder

49

Pantie Elastic When the stitched-on wide elastic around the tops of panties or half slips has lost its elasticity, it can of course be replaced. Remember to stretch it when sewing it on; it is also advisable to use a long stitch when sewing on elastic, even when using your zigzag stitch. It is probably easier, however, after snipping the elastic off, to baste in a narrow hem around the top, turn a half-inch hem, and run through a quarter-inch-wide strip of elastic, cut to your waist measure, to hold it up thereafter.

Mending Brassieres   Well-fitting brassieres are expensive and worth careful repair. If yours no longer gives support, examine it thoroughly to see what is wrong.

A good brassiere is made of strong material that is likely to outlast in usefulness the elastic with which it is combined. It is well worth while to replace the stretched elastic. Working carefully, making sure the raw ends of the elastic are covered with the brassiere material or with bias tape, you can completely hide the fact that the brassiere has been repaired.

Experiment first with pins and tucks to see what changes will restore its fit. Do not cut away anything until you are sure you have found the place that needs tightening or replacing. Even then, does it need to be cut? Take a tuck in the place that you think is too loose and hold your tuck with a safety pin, or baste it, while you try the brassiere on.

Remember that it is usually the elastic that gives way. Which strip of elastic was it? Stitched-on elastic around the lower part of the brassiere may resemble lace so closely that you do not realize it is an integral part of the fitting and supporting function of the brassiere, and when this lower elastic stretches, it is not at once apparent what has happened. To distinguish it from the strong, heavy elastic, it is here called "lace elastic;" it could as well be called "thin elastic."

Having taken tucks and pinned them and tried the brassiere on repeatedly, you can decide what is needed and go ahead. Stitched-on lace elastic is not usually too thick in structure; you can often take up its slack with a series of little tucks or darts. It is also not too difficult to replace the lacelike elastic. After practicing with pinned-in tucks until the fit is right, as has been said, measure the tucked-to-fit edge and cut a strip of fresh lace elastic of this length. Remove the pinned tucks and remove the old, stretched lace elastic. Pin the new lace elastic at the ends, where it will be covered, usually, by the bias tape that covered the ends of the old elastic. Stretch the new elastic to the length of the material and pin it at intervals to this lower edge of the brassiere. Then stitch it in place, stretching the elastic to fit as you stitch.

There are places where no elastic was sewed on and where the material and its bias facing have stretched; this also can well be repaired by removing the bias-tape facing and substituting lace elastic, ascertaining the right fit by tucks and fitting and measuring as outlined above.

When the strong, heavy elastic that performed a main function in the fitting and supporting has lost its stretch (Fig. 50a), it should be replaced. Snip it out very carefully; see every stitch you cut, lest you cut some threads of the material itself. (Fig. 50b.) Cut your new elastic to fit, and, again, pin or baste your changes in place and try the brassiere on. When it feels right, sew in the new elastic on the right side (Fig. 50c), then turn to the wrong side and hem down the binding that covered the raw ends of the elastic on the wrong side. Take it to your sewing machine and, on the wrong side, stitch the binding in place. (Fig. 50d.) Turn to the right side and stitch the hemmed edge there also. (Fig. 50e.) It is best to use a long stitch when sewing on elastic, and be sure to stretch it when that is called for.

When the strip to which the hooks and eyes are attached is worn out, in an otherwise good brassiere, you can of course make a new one, but, curiously,

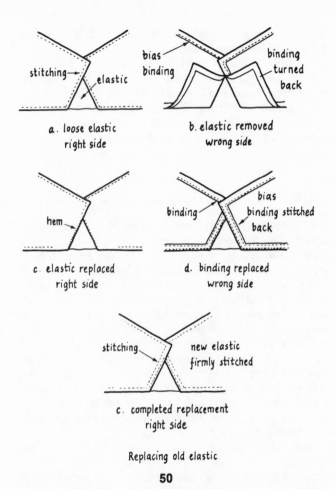

a. loose elastic
right side

stitching — elastic

b. elastic removed
wrong side

bias binding

binding turned back

c. elastic replaced
right side

hem

d. binding replaced
wrong side

binding

bias binding stitched back

c. completed replacement
right side

stitching

new elastic firmly stitched

Replacing old elastic

50

this is a place that is difficult to mend neatly. Happily, new tape fastenings to replace this strip can be purchased at notion counters.

Put aside any strips of the fresh elastic left over from your brassiere mending. Someday you may want to use it to replace the elastic of this recent mend, on this same brassiere.

Garters Elastic garters are to be replaced on foundation garments much as elastic is sewed on brassieres, hemming the material over the edge of the elastic and hemming the bias tape down over the raw edges on the back. Stitch back and forth a few times on the machine to hold them more firmly.

WORK CLOTHING_____

The problem here is only to achieve a firm, useful mend. The mended area should appear strongly and neatly mended but you needn't try very hard to hide the fact that the garment has been repaired.

Be especially sure to examine the whole garment thoroughly before starting any mending. Holes in the elbow are easily overlooked and are difficult to mend. Are the cuffs and the lower edges of the garment frayed? Is there a tear hidden in some fold? Be sure the zippers work efficiently. Are you sure you can mend the garment well enough so that the owner will wear it again? If you must buy repair materials, as buttons, zippers and ironed-on patches, will the mended garment be worth the expense and the work you have put into it?

Sometimes, under unusual conditions, it turns out that the owner badly wants a worn garment rehabilitated. A husband may think certain golf pants or his fisherman's coat brings him luck, or a boy insist that his mother patch his favorite plaid pants instead of discarding and replacing them.

A large proportion of the work clothing to be mended will usually be of blue denim. This fades unevenly where it is worn or exposed, so blue denim patches of different shades can look more or less as if they belonged where they are. If you have more than one wearer of blue denim in your family, it would certainly be worthwhile to save all discards for use as patching materials.

Repair ragged knees with cemented-on patches. Either use matching material and try to make the patches unobtrusive or use large rectangular patches of similar material and let them show. Small holes or tears may be mended with small cemented patches matching the original material as closely as possible.

Replace every missing button. Try out the zipper. Sew up ripped seams. Remember to use the heavy machine needle.

Stitch loosened pockets with strong thread or stitch the seam twice. A simple stitched-on pocket can be replaced by one of matching material. If you use non-matching material, replace the pockets on both sides, whether the second one needs replacement or not.

If a small worn place in a pocket can be mended easily with a cemented-on patch, place a thickness of newspaper in the pocket (so the two sides do not get cemented together) and paste the patch on. If the pocket is not easily mended thus, make new ones. (See "Pockets.")

When the oversized hook and eye that is now so often used to fasten waistbands has pulled loose, it is possible to pry up the prongs, mend and reinforce the place in the waistband where the hook (it is usually the hook that has torn loose) was, push the prongs back through and pinch them back into place. The prongs should not go through to the outside of the band, where they would show, so you mend the inner, underneath part of the waistband, put the hook in place and hem the upper part of the band down again. Of course, if you prefer, at notion counters you can buy new oversized hooks and eyes that can be sewed on.

Replacing a Belt Loop   Belt loops frequently pull loose at the upper end, where the loop was sewed, in between the top of the pants and the inside lining of the belt. To replace a loop begin by snipping the loop entirely loose from the pants, which means cutting the short little stitches that held the lower end of the loop to the pants. Pull out all the loose ends of stitches.

You are going to replace the loop so that it will look exactly as it did when the pants were new, so straighten out the loop and poke its upper end in between pants and lining, where it was formerly attached. Stitch it firmly in place, sewing through the pants material, the hidden upper end of the loop and the belt lining inside. Preferably, use several rows of machine stitching.

Then bend the loop back down over your recent stitching and replace its lower end exactly where it was before. Sew it into place with back and forth stitching. Since this stitching shows plainly, use either thread matching the color of the material or else transparent or dark single filament nylon thread.

Fly-to-Crotch Mend   That miserable little place between the lower end of the zipper and the crotch, in men's pants, is a frequent source of trouble. There is a strain here and stitches and material give way. (Fig. 51a.) Pull the parts back together, and study how the parts and the stitching went in the first place. In planning the mending, keep in mind that the area is so far down toward the crotch that the mending will not be too evident.

If there is only the problem of stitching that has given way, pin or baste the edges back in their original position, and restitch everything carefully back into place. It is often best basting a patch of thin

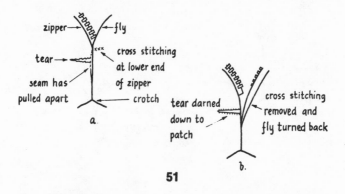

51

but firm material underneath and stitching down to this, then catching the edges of the patch to the material. This is another place where the outside edges of the patch have a considerable tendency to fold over and get stitched in twice; look out for this.

If edges of the material have pulled or torn loose and reinforcement is a necessity, find patching material of firmly woven cloth and hem and darn the edges of the material down to the patch, not turning under the edges of the material, except for loose stitches. Stitch the darn to the patch with machine darning, preferably with transparent or dark single-filament nylon thread.

You may find that this is easier to direct than to do in the confined space you have to work in. You may have to snip the stitching that holds the fold of the material over the lower end of the zipper and completely loosen the material in that area. Open the zipper, too. (Fig. 51b.)

Having sewed each edge of the seam to its patch material, cut the seam edge of the patch to conform to the original seam edges of the pants, and baste and hem everything into its original arrangement. (Fig. 51c.) This will include reconstituting

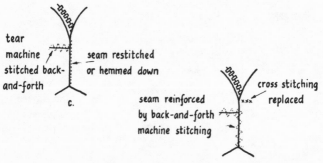

tear

machine stitched back-and-forth

seam restitched or hemmed down

c.

seam reinforced by back-and-forth machine stitching

cross stitching replaced

Fly-to-crotch mend

the seam across the lower end of the fly if you had to take out those stitches. (Fig. 51d.)

Restitch where the machine stitches went in the original stitching. When sewing across the end of the fly, proceed stitch by stitch, trying not to stitch through the lowest teeth of the zipper.

While you can appreciate that it is preferable to use self material for the patch, it usually seems as if quite a large piece of material is going to be needed, larger than any small piece of self material you can find that can be spared from its original location. You choose, therefore, patch material matching the pants material as closely as possible. Put the patch under the ragged and torn side, and pin the pants material on that side to the patch, as nearly as possible to the way it was arranged before. Pin the torn edge in place on it, to make sure that the two sides can eventually be restitched together without undue puckering on either side.

Having accomplished this, stop and look again at the size of the bit of patch that still shows. You will see that the section of patch that shows now is not such a big space after all. On the other hand, you may note that the bit of patch that still shows is more evident than you had thought it would be. That tear extended out and up, following the weave of the cloth.

Look again for a small replacement patch of self material, the size of the little bit that shows. Often, it can be found right there, almost underneath where you are working. It is in the protecting length of self material under the zipper itself, extending from the belt to the lower end of the zipper and a little further. Cut off the bit you need and use it in the patch. Replace it by a corresponding piece of material of the same strength, unless the protection was double, when you can cut what you need from the double material and overcast the raw edges that remain.

Before cutting the second patch, plan its placement. This can be done in two ways.

First, tuck the bit of self material under the ragged edge of the tear. Baste it in place, onto the first patch, poke the ragged edges of the pants back underneath and carefully hem these ragged edges down over and onto this new patch of self material. Crisscross over the edges with back-and-forth machine stitching, using transparent or dark nylon thread. Then, as directed earlier, pin or baste the rest of the edges back onto the original patch, hem everything back into place and restitch.

The second method has only a slight modification. Instead of using the self material as an underneath patch, use it as a modified "inset" patch. Hem the edges of the pants down to the original patch, then fold and baste under the edges of the little self-material patch until you have a patch that exactly fits into the place where the material of the first patch shows. Baste the self-material patch into this (like fitting a piece of a jigsaw puzzle into place), and hem it there, right against the edges of the pants material. Then, again, stitch back and forth across the hemmed edges, and occasionally across the new patch, with transparent or dark nylon thread. Hem the other edges in place and stitch the two sides together again.

This second method has the advantage that it can be used when, as occasionally happens, you discover only after you think you have a good mend that your first patch shows too much. Without cutting anything out, you can add the inset patch right over the bit of the first patch that shows.

It doesn't hurt the appearance at all if you start with a non-matching patch underneath and end up covering it, what of it showed, with a bit of self material.

Once, faced with such a problem, and thinking that she had no self material that could be spared, one mending lady took the tools of another calling and applied to her too-bright patch a thin wash of artists' ochre-colored paint. This "antiquing" worked out fine; the patch now blended inconspicuously with the faded garment material.

For an interested and fairly experienced mender, the fly-to-crotch mend is not as hard as it sounds and the results usually look much better than expected.

DRESSES_____

Now consider hiding conspicuous mends on good clothing. Think, for instance, of a hole, a spot, a tear on the front of a good dress. Study the problem with care, noting any ideas that occur to you and then, perhaps, laying them aside while you look up other possibilities. Visit shops and dress departments.

You should try hard to make your correction look as if it had been an original part of the garment. Be careful; it is easy to overdo the cover-up and have a too-ornamented dress. Except for children's clothing, keep the effect as simple as possible.

Think of little folds, little darts and tucks, rows of tiny buttons. Consider, even, pinned-on sets of costume jewelry, though this would break one almost invariable rule; that you do not purchase any new material to mend used garments.

A tear in the front in the midline can be made into a buttoned placket. Consider a neck binding in self color or in a contrasting color. For a tear down one side of a neck opening, close with a dart and make another on the other side, to give the idea that the designer chose that method of securing fullness in the blouse.

If your garment is "sporty" enough in effect to stand it, a pocket of contrasting material or even of leather might be an excellent cover-up. Another pocket on the other side of the front of the dress? When any new material is added, the completed effect may appear "busy," or even "fussy." You may have to remove any decoration already on the dress as a correction.

In rough-finished fabrics, a woven-in mending of self material might well be used for problems such as a small burned hole in the front of a dress.

Concerning skirt mending specifically, can a tear be taken into a seam or can a new seam be constructed, waist to bottom, to contain the tear? Depending on where the mend is or where it can be moved to, can pleats be drawn together over it, stitching them down?

If the garment is worth the effort, you can take the skirt off the blouse and shift the mend or the fresh seam to the side or the back. You would of course have to adjust the length and do the bottom hem over.

When you need to enlarge a waistband, for some of us do put on weight sometimes, you will want to extend both the outside belt, usually of the same material as the rest of the garment, and the inside waistband, usually of some strong material and not of the garment material.

To extend the outside belt, change the location of the button—or the eye of the hook and eye, if that is the fastening. Now for the inside band. It is nearly always fastened by a hook and eye, just above the upper edge of the zipper end. If your projected extension is going to make this opening gape too widely to be bridged by the existing hook and eye, snip back the belt from the waistband for an inch or two, lengthen the waistband by a fold of material, such as doubled tape or, better, doubled elastic, and sew the hook onto its outer end. (Fig. 52.)

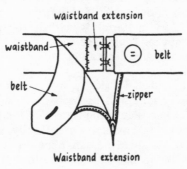

Waistband extension

52

To extend a fabric belt, turn under each end of the belt one inch, forming a loop. Secure a yard and a half to two yards of ornamental cord, cut it in two, run half the cord through each loop and tie knots in the ends. Pull the cords to even lengths on each side, draw the belt to fit and tie the cords in a bowknot in the center front. (Fig. 53.)

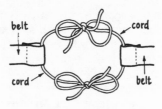

Belt extension

53

To lengthen the belt of a simple, washable dress, you can even use a pair of long white shoelaces to draw up the ends of the belt. In a more pretentious dress, the cord ends could be weighed down by large metal beads threaded into the ends.

For garments that will be dry cleaned, such as wool skirts, belt extensions can be cut and shaped from leather and fastened with buckles.

COATS._____

The problem is that we deal with thick material, perhaps even with stiff plastic, in outside, conspicuous and sometimes expensive garments.

When a coat needs to be shortened, study its make-up, observing the process that was used in places such as where the front facing meets the bottom hem. Here a thickness has to be cut away to reduce the bulkiness in that corner edge. When taking up the hem, reproduce the original procedure. Then, having put in as neat a hem as you can, press it very carefully or hire a tailor to press it, for the final effect depends to quite an extent on the pressing. If the coat is valuable, it may be better to take it to a tailor or professional dressmaker for the alteration.

Seams When a seam has given way in a coat, it must be restitched from the inside, as it was stitched in the first place. If you try to mend it from the outside, almost invariably the effect is a sort of hem—the stitches show.

To restitch it from the inside, if the garment is lined, you must somehow get inside that lining. Examine the coat to see if the bottom hem is not loosely hand stitched in place or even only tacked down here and there.

It is more difficult to get inside the lining when the stitching goes through to the outside, as often occurs in sport coats. Here coat and lining are joined under a line of bias tape, one edge of which is stitched to the coat, the other to the lining. (Fig. 54.) A little

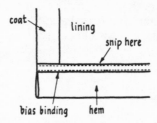

Tape closed bottom hem

54

study will show you which line of stitching goes through all thicknesses, from the inside of the lining to the outside of the coat. This is the one line of stitching to snip. It is usually the upper line of stitching. Snipping it frees the lining.

After you have completed stitching the seams or doing any other mending that had to be done from the inside, replace and restitch the lining. First, however, pin the hem back exactly the same width it was before. In any but very firm material, it is very easy to take in a hem wider than the previous one. Then tuck the lining back under the upper edge of the bias tape, pin or baste the parts into place and restitch through the upper edge of the bias tape, the lining and the coat material.

Sew this carefully; frequently lift up the coat hem and look at your stitching from the outside. Sometimes, through weeks or months of wear, extra outside material has folded itself down over the former line of stitching and unless you look out it will fold itself down again and will slip a bit of doubled material down into your line of restitching. It will help to push the redundant coat material back up and pin it out of the way.

Too often, it is the seam in the lining nearest the outside seam to be mended that must be widely opened. Even then it may not be possible to restitch the seam, if the material is thick and heavy, on the sewing machine. It must be restitched by hand. Use strong thread, and backstitch it. When restitching coats of plastic material, you will usually have to hand stitch the outside seams.

Do not reclose any lining seams you have opened until you are sure you do not need the seam opening to reach and mend some other place in the coat. Also, do not take your matching thread off the sewing machine until you are sure you are through stitching.

Ordinarily, if the material has torn or pulled away from a seam, the injured edge must be mended and reinforced. Probably a reinforcing patch should be put underneath as well. In an area such as under the arm, or the seam areas near it, mending like this does not show badly. Here the area to be mended may well be cemented down to a thin but strong material, which should be of a matching color if it will show at all. The very edge, where coat is cemented to patch, probably should take back-and-forth stitching. Cut the seam edges of the patch to the seam line of the garment, baste the two edges of the garment together and stitch.

Other Mends If an elbow has given way while the rest of the coat is still good, again, remember that leather elbow patches do not look bad on sport coats. To stitch them in place, the sleeve lining seams will have to be widely opened, but perhaps you can cement them on with fabric cement. When stitching leather, remember to use a heavy, strong sewing machine needle.

If the edges of your coat show wear while the general surface seems still good, the edges can be bound with braid. That coat could then no longer be "best" wear, but it could still be plenty good enough for city shopping.

When your fur coat, growing older and more brittle, splits somewhere, it is not too difficult to mend, for the fur on the outside can hide the mending. You will have to get inside the lining, usually by snipping the lining from the bottom of the coat. Then bring the torn edges of the skin together. Press and poke every bit of fur to the outside and hand sew the two edges together just as they went together in the first place. Use strong thread and sew six or eight stitches to the inch.

Then reinforce the seam with a strip of strong material and fabric cement. Before applying the cement, examine the inside skin surface to see if it is covered with a glaze. If it is, this must be scraped off, else the fabric cement will only adhere to the glaze and the patch will soon come loose.

When you have finished the mend, sew the lining to the bottom of the coat again.

WINDBREAKERS_____

Our mending committee had considerable practice in mending men's and boys' windbreakers. The mending of their cuffs, collars, pockets and zippers has been taken up already. Here you will learn the treatment of some of the problems peculiar to windbreakers.

They do not have rigid rules for their workmanship or decoration, so you have a good deal of leeway for improvisation as you search for a way to mend the garment and think of how it will look when it is done.

Seams One of the most difficult problems is the windbreaker whose thin nylon material has pulled apart at some seam (or at several seams) with or without breaking the seam threads themselves. This leaves a long fringe of the pulled nylon threads. Some of the threads may still be sewed into the seam itself, at their tips. (Fig. 55a.)

First of all, you look the garment over carefully to see whether it is worth saving. Often it is, for this seam pulling can occur while lining, zipper and cuffs are still in excellent condition.

The solution will leave a little upstanding seam. You had best use nylon thread, for cotton thread would be cheap-looking here. If, as often happens, the windbreaker is dark in color, black nylon thread is preferable to transparent.

If the nylon threads have pulled from both sides of the seam, open the seam and cut back the fringe to about a third of an inch. Pull out and discard every bit of the detached fringe. (Fig. 55b.) Now

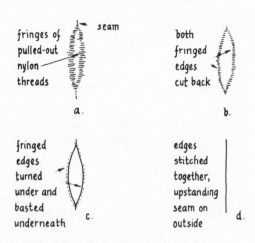

fringes of pulled-out nylon threads ← seam	both fringed edges cut back
a.	b.
fringed edges turned under and basted underneath c.	edges stitched together, upstanding seam on outside d.

Repair of nylon seam, both edges ragged

55

painstakingly baste the raw edges under, on each side, making tiny hems. (Fig. 55c.) Be sure every thread of the fringe is caught under. This is the most exasperating part of the mend; you may have to run your basting thread through more than once to catch down all those fine, wiry fringe threads. Finally, baste the two edges together and machine stitch together in a narrow hem, using a short stitch on the machine and loosening its tension. (Fig. 55d.)

Sometimes only one side is pulled from the seam. This occurs usually when the other side is backed by firm, strong material. It often happens when the material pulls from a pocket stitching. (Fig. 56a.) Again, cut the pulled fringe to about a third of an inch (Fig. 56b.) and baste the pulled end underneath (Fig. 56c.). Then hem this edge down to the seam. (Instead of making the edges into an upstanding seam, as was done before.) (Fig. 56d.) Your stitching must be close and firm, and it is a good idea to go over the edge twice, back and forth. It is rarely possible to stitch this place on the machine.

If well done, the windbreaker looks well enough to wear on the playground, and the child will probably be willing to wear it to school. It may do for informal skiing. But if several prominent seams have been restitched, it can hardly be recommended for wear at a ski resort.

At the moment, fashion sanctions strips of contrasting material stitched over the long outside seams of sportswear. If they can be put on without too much sweat and tears, they could beautifully hide places where the material has pulled out from the seams. One could cement on a strip of braid, the ends of which would have to be hidden in body seams or in hems. Stitched-on strips would hide frayed seams

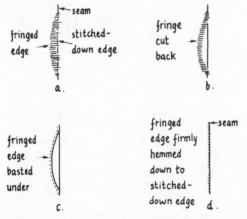

Repair of nylon seam, one edge ragged

56

exceptionally well, but it is to be feared that taking out the lining seams to get at the outside seams properly would mean all but remaking the windbreaker.

Hoods   Windbreakers often have attached hoods. If the outside seam of the hood has given way, open the lining seam to restitch it from the inside, for these seams are conspicuous.

A badly torn hood (Fig. 57a) can be mended by putting new material all over it, outside, hemming down all the edges to the seam line just in from face and neck (Fig. 57b). If a hood is too small, a wide band can be put about the face to widen the hood.

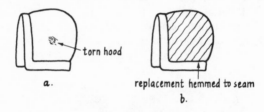

a.

replacement hemmed to seam

b.

Repair of torn windbreaker hood

57

If, as often happens, the cord that runs inside the front edge of the hood, to tie it closely about the face, is gone, secure a yard of cord to replace it. The problem here is, usually, threading it through the often too-small eyelets. Thread string into an oversized darning needle, and with a fine thread firmly sew the end of the string into the end of your cord. (Fig. 58a.) Leave on the darning needle a length of string equal to the needle's own length. Now thread the eye end of the needle through the eyelet of the hood

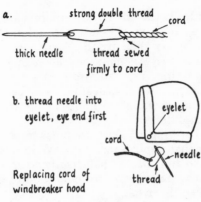

a. strong double thread cord

thick needle thread sewed
firmly to cord

b. thread needle into
eyelet, eye end first eyelet

cord

needle

Replacing cord of thread
windbreaker hood

58

and use this method to pull the cord through. (Fig. 58b.) Cut off the sewed bit and tie firm knots in the ends of the cord.

If the metal eyelet is gone, there is a gadget to replace metal eyelets. Be sure to bring any frayed edges together (with transparent or dark nylon thread, preferably) before you put in the new metal eyelets. If your buttonholer is easy to put in place and use, remember that there is an eyelet template among the buttonholer patterns. Again, mend the frayed eyelet before you use the buttonholer template. Since the eyelet only goes through the surface material of the hood, you will have to snip open the nearest seam enough to get the surface material out where you can work on it with either the metal eyelet gadget or the sewing machine.

Other Mends An unusual repair idea that may come in handy, when a conspicuous place in a windbreaker must be mended, is to insert a short zipper and pretend there is a pocket there. One finds such short zipper pockets in outlandish places on windbreakers today—on the outside of the upper sleeve, for instance.

For little holes in boys' windbreaker jackets, cement on small patches of material matching in color but thicker than nylon. These will show and they are not easy to apply and keep in place until they start drying. You can also hem down the edges of the hole to an underneath patch, but this will usually mean opening the lining at the bottom hem or near the place to be mended.

If the covering of the windbreaker is of nylon, remember that you can rarely if at all iron on a patch or strip. An iron heated sufficiently to melt the adhesive in the patch or strip would tend to crinkle or actually melt the nylon.

The Lining When the problem is one of mending the lining of the windbreaker, look carefully to see if the coat is reversible, as windbreakers often are; if it is, more care must be used in closing a seam. Look at the zipper slide; in a reversible coat there are heavy pull tabs on both sides of the zipper slides.

Rather too frequently, the lowest one to three inches of the lining of a windbreaker wears through. Since a soft cotton interlining often shows, this can be especially unsightly. (Fig. 59a.) If the worn area is a narrow one just above the hem, you can make a quick and good repair by cutting off the ragged edge all the way across and shortening the garment half an inch or so. To do this, carefully snip the seam that joins hem and lining. (Fig. 59b.) If they were joined by a bias binding, snip the upper stitching of the binding, the one that stitches through binding, lining and coat material. Then cut off the inch or so of worn lining (Fig. 59c) and turn the windbreaker material up. If there is not over an inch of worn material to be discarded, you will be increasing the width of the hem by about half an inch. (Fig. 59d.) If you have to discard more ragged lining, you will be increasing the width of the hem proportionately.

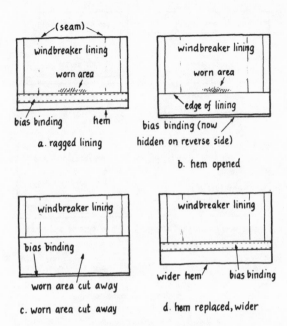

a. ragged lining

b. hem opened

c. worn area cut away

d. hem replaced, wider

Windbreaker shortened to cover worn area

59

Lift the bias tape over the lining, over the cut-off edge, and restitch.

If there was no bias binding—if lining and windbreaker were stitched directly to each other, usually at very bottom edge of the windbreaker (Fig. 60a)— snip them apart, cut off the strip of worn lining (Fig. 60b), and baste a bias binding to the lower edge of the windbreaker itself. Place the right sides of binding and windbreaker together and stitch the bias binding to the windbreaker edge, running the stitching just outside the former line of stitching. (Fig. 60c.)

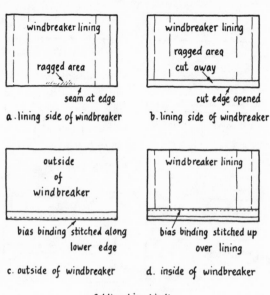

a. lining side of windbreaker

seam at edge

windbreaker lining

ragged area

b. lining side of windbreaker

cut edge opened

windbreaker lining

ragged area
cut away

c. outside of windbreaker

bias binding stitched along lower edge

outside
of
windbreaker

d. inside of windbreaker

bias binding stitched up over lining

windbreaker lining

Adding bias binding

60

You now have a bias binding on the windbreaker, so repeat the last procedure, lifting the binding up over the edge of the lining, pinning or basting it and stitching right through binding, lining and windbreaker. Be sure the hem is even in width all the way across. (Fig. 60d.)

If a wider area is worn through above the bottom edge (Fig. 61a), you will need to replace this by a long, wide patch. To look good, the whole strip of worn lining, from one back seam to the other or, even better, from one coat front to the other, should be replaced by a long, neat patch.

Decide how much of the lining must be sacrificed, measure this width from the bottom of the lining and mark this width, by pins or basting, all the way across the lower part of the lining. (Fig. 61b.) Cut a patch, of color and material matching the old lining as closely as possible, and an inch wider than the width of lining to be sacrificed, and stitch it to the old lining along your marked line, right sides together, the patch material pushed up toward the upper part of the windbreaker. (Fig. 61c.)

Bring the patch down over the worn lining, adjust the length of the patch to the length of the old lining and cut the patch, if you need to, the same length the old lining was. And now, at last, you can cut away the worn strip of lining, leaving, of course, a half inch or so next to the seam. Press this seam open. (Fig. 61d.)

Bring the hem of the windbreaker up over the lower edge of the patch and baste the edge of the bias binding to the lower edge of the patch. (If there was no binding on the edge of the windbreaker material, stitch one on, following the instruction just given.)

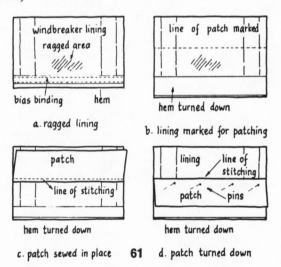

a. ragged lining

b. lining marked for patching

c. patch sewed in place   **61**   d. patch turned down

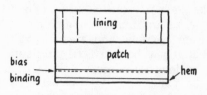

e. hem stitched up over patch

Patching bottom of lining of windbreaker

Now stitch it, through binding, patch and material. (Fig. 61e.) As noted earlier, be sure the hem in the material, on the right side, is of even width from one side to the other. Take all the precautions for this as directed in "Coats." The stitching shows on the outside, the right side, and the lower edge of the windbreaker will not look good if the hem is irregular in width.

6

OTHER
PROBLEMS

KNIT MATERIALS_____

Mending knit clothing, whether hand knit or machine knit, is not easy. The looped structure is difficult to duplicate with a needle; a crochet hook can do little more. It is all but impossible to persuade a darn to look like anything but a darn in a knit fabric.

Occasionally one can cover such a mend with a disguise, and some parts of hand knits can be re-knit, but in general you come to think, ruefully, that knits may be wonderful, but not when it comes to mending them.

Matching yarns to mend any woolens (or manmade wool-like fabrics) is always a problem. Today, many women do crewel embroidery, and if you have a friend who does, she may be willing to spare a strand for some special mending. You can also buy packets of mending yarn in shops or departments that specialize in supplies for those of us who sew.

In any knit garment, examine first the place where the shoulder seam meets the neck seam. This is a point of strain; the seams give way easily and the edges fray, so it is hard to put in a mend that does not show. You have to mend the stitching of both shoulder and neck, by hand or machine. It would be wise to inspect this area in a newly purchased garment and reinforce it if the stitching seems at all insecure.

You can mend a tiny hole by bringing together the edges of the material over it and running fine thread of a matching color about under the surface, where it can to some extent be kept from showing.

How about mending close-knit and stretch materials? Like all knitted fabrics—like sweaters, mittens, stockings and socks—they are difficult to mend. However, these modern materials have so fine a stitch and are so thick, they can sometimes be handled like a thick woven fabric—say, a tweed (which is also hard to mend). Follow the directions in the section "Specific Places and Problems."

• Patching Knit Materials
The Darned-to-a-Patch Mend A slashed hole, as a sharp little cut or a small corner tear, in a close-knit fabric can sometimes be quite well mended, if the mender is willing to put in some time and effort. (Fig. 62a.)

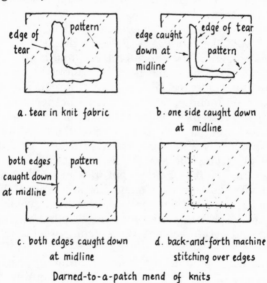

a. tear in knit fabric

b. one side caught down at midline

c. both edges caught down at midline

d. back-and-forth machine stitching over edges

Darned-to-a-patch mend of knits

62

Put a patch, of firm material and matching color, under the material. If even a small patch of the garment material is available, use that under the opening, tacked over the firm patch if necessary. (However, knit garments often have few or no bits of the garment material available.)

Pin the material to the patch. If the edges of the hole are gaping, bring these together. If there is a pattern in the material, reconstruct it. Then with transparent or dark single-filament nylon thread, pick up each tiny loop and line of thread along the edge and bring it to the middle of the patch and catch it down. (Fig. 62b.) On the opposite side of the tear, do the same, bringing the loops and threads on both sides together, covering the surface of the patch. (Fig. 62c.) You may find you are puckering the knit material a little; never mind, it is supposed to be able to stretch.

If you have done this mend carefully, it may seem to be completely and well mended as it is. It will wear better, however, if you machine stitch back and forth across the mended line with single-filament nylon thread. (Fig. 62d.)

Underneath, cut the patch edges to within half an inch of the stitching and catch them down loosely to the material.

This is by no means an invisible mend, but if the threads have entirely covered the patch, it will do for such garments as a child's playsuit or dress.

Inset Patch If there must be an open patch, the inset patch, very carefully done, put in with transparent or dark nylon thread, offers the best chance of success. Remember to catch down the edges of the knit material underneath. If the pattern is perfectly matched and the final pressing thorough and well done, it does not show very much. Knits are too thick for ordinary patching.

The "Baggy" Knit As you well know, knit fabrics —again, like tweeds—tend to stretch out of shape with age and wear. Sometimes the dry cleaner can more or less get them back into good form, but by the time such a garment is stretched and worn at points of wear, it is hard to see how they can possibly be mended to look "as good as new" again.

The best treatment for a baggy knit skirt is prevention. That is, select a skirt (or, if you are making it, a pattern) that takes advantage of the stretchiness of the material; it should have no openings at the sides but should be held up by a strong elastic at the top. Such a skirt is slipped on over the head or pulled up from the feet. Since it has no definite back or front, it can be turned around and the places of wear more equalized.

Sweaters Examine the whole sweater, detail by detail. In hardly any other class of garments is it so often hard to decide whether or not the one you have in your hand is worth mending. A woman's sweater that has lost its chic is likely to be a sloppy-appearing affair. A man's sweater, on the other hand, probably because it is so much heavier, may stand careful and concealed mends and still be quite useful.

Pick up runs with a crochet hook, holding each final loop with a safety pin or the stitch holder from your knitting bag.

Reknitting is not often enough considered. Reknitting the frayed end of a finger in a black wool glove could make an especially good mend.

The Scotswoman who was the original of Effie Deans in Scott's *The Heart of Midlothian,* is quoted as having said that in winter she "footed stockings" —that is, knit feet to country people's worn stockings, and Jo March, in *Little Women,* knit heels into the worn socks of Professor Bhaer, whom she afterward married. It would be difficult in today's machine-knit socks, matted by repeated washings, to pick up the stitches to reknit the heels. The stitches would be more easily picked up if the socks were hand knitted, no doubt. In most sweaters, on the other hand, the stitches can rather easily be picked up again.

For ragged cuffs, ravel both cuffs back to the main sleeve stitches. Tie up and wash the raveled yarn. Reknit the cuffs, adding stripes of a suitable color to make up for the discarded original yarn. Then sew these reknit cuffs to the sleeve edges as described in the last part of "Cuffs." Then, in a child's sweater especially, the garment will look better if some of the added yarn is used for an ornament elsewhere, as for a gathering cord ending in a couple of pompons at the neck.

What is to be done when the sleeve of a sweater has worn through while the rest of the sweater shows no need of repair? If you can get pieces of leather big enough, put on leather patches. I have seen heavy sweaters, quite new, worn by well-to-do young men, with large leather patches on the sleeves.

Now I will suggest a mend I have never had the opportunity to try out—something I do not often do. Reknit the sleeve from just above the ragged elbow. Mark, on both the worn and the good sleeve, the place to which you will ravel the worn sleeve, for you will be using the good sleeve as a pattern. Then ravel the worn sleeve back from the cuff edge to your mark, keeping the elbow strands separate, for you must not knit them into the elbow section again; use them in a part of the sleeve that will get less wear. Ravel out the cuff of the good sleeve as well.

Wind the yarn in loose coils tied four times to prevent tangling; wash the yarn, dry it and reknit the sleeve. It may be best to first knit a little sample, perhaps three inches square to see if your needles are the correct size to duplicate the stitches-per-inch of the rest of the sweater.

By the time you come to the cuffs, you will notice a need for more yarn, to replace what you lost in the worn-out elbow. Add in yarn of another color as stripes in the cuffs, and possibly in ornaments elsewhere in the sweater, as I directed for the reknitting of worn cuffs.

Reconstituted Knitting Stitches   In more than one book, directions are given for reconstituting a badly worn place or an actual hole in a knitted article of clothing by reinforcing or copying and continuing the knitting stitches by means of a needle threaded with matching yarn. I tried hard to follow these directions but could never achieve a good result. It looked "mended." Since, however, others have apparently found the methods useful, I will describe them.

To reinforce a place where an area has worn very thin, you thread your needle with yarn matching in color but preferably smaller than that in the garment you are mending. With your yarn-threaded needle, follow each strand of the original garment across, up through a loop, down around the neck of the loop below, back up the surface and down through your first loop again. Then bring your needle up through the next adjacent loop and so on, across the thin area and back, until the whole area is reinforced. (Fig. 63a.)

My sample was certainly reinforced, but it looked added to and mended.

To fill a hole in a knitted garment is a much more complicated procedure. First, you cut the hole to a rectangle and hem back the cut yarn at the sides. Then you run a fine thread up and down, through a loop in one corner at the top of the hole, down through the corresponding loop at the bottom of the hole and up and down until all the loops are connected. (Fig. 63b.) Then with your yarn-threaded needle, you rework the missing loops; bring the yarn up through a loop (probably the first one you ran the fine thread through), down under and around the threads stretched down from it, up to the surface again and down through your loop, up through the next one and so on, over to the hemmed-down sides and back and forth until the hole is covered. (Fig. 63c.)

Mine looked mended. I did another and it was neater but still did not look as if it had all been part of the original garment. In addition, there was the fact that the hole had been in the middle of a wide worn area, and the difference in appearance between the worn area and my reconstituted patch showed conspicuously.

I have not discoursed so long about these methods purely to condemn them. Apparently, sometime, somewhere, they have been found useful. It may be

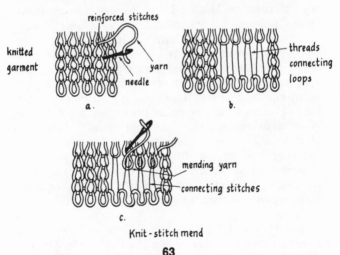

Knit - stitch mend

63

that in times when clothing was mended and worn and mended and worn repeatedly, women in the homes mended knitted articles so much and so often that they became expert at it and their knitted mends did not look so sad as did my amateur work.

So, if you are a pioneer or for some other reason have to husband your possessions with extra care, start to learn and practice, and I offer you hope of improvement. Even my own attempts looked better as I persisted.

BLANKETS_____

Some people mend their blankets until their relatives start apologizing for them. Others give away blankets that only need fresh bindings.

If the bindings are worn, remove them. This can often be easily done, for they are usually held by several rows of "lock stitch," which can be taken out by pulling at a thread at one end. (See "General Notes" as to pulling out chain stitch.)

Then, if your blanket is a good one, think of additional possibilities for improvement before going on. You can, of course, simply rebind it, purchasing ready-cut and folded binding and stitching it on. Wide bindings are not necessities; they are a matter of convention, like the three-inch hems at the tops of sheets. You can make your own, if you prefer, by securing half or two-thirds of a yard of yard-wide material. First, shrink it well. Then cut it in four equal lengths and stitch each two lengths together, right sides together, to go on the two ends of the blanket.

The blanket binding is put on just as bias binding is sewed onto the edge of any fabric. That is, you can sew one side down, right sides together (Fig. 64a),

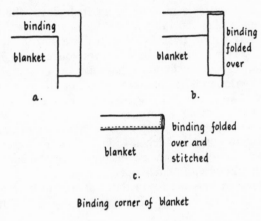

Binding corner of blanket

64

fold the rest of the binding over to the other side of the blanket (Fig. 64b), turn a small hem and stitch it down (Fig. 64c). As an alternative, you can try to make the binding the same width on both sides of the blanket (as you would be doing if you used ready-folded purchased blanket bindings) and stitch through both edges of the bindings.

When turning under the binding at the ends, tuck in the corner of the blanket itself under one of the folds and run your stitching over the binding edges to the corner.

If you wish, instead of holding the raw edges of the blanket with a fabric binding, you can keep them from raveling with a hand-embroidered edge stitch, the obviously named "blanket stitch." To blanket stitch, you have only to bring your needle out at the edge of the blanket over your thread. To hold the edge firmly, your stitches may need to be fairly close, about eight stitches to the inch. They look good in groups of three, of graduating depth. For this, take the first stitch a quarter of an inch deep, the next three-eighths, the third a half inch, and repeat. You can buy cotton floss for this in dime stores. Or you may prefer to use up bits of floss you already have.

Blanket Extensions A housekeeper does not like it when one of her blankets does not "tuck in" well. A good wool blanket, for instance, may have shrunk badly in repeated washings.

A satisfactory correction is to stitch an extension, twelve to eighteen inches wide, across the lower end of the blanket. Such extension material should be shrunk before it is made up.

If extensions are also needed at the sides, they are ordinarily made to go all the way up (Fig. 65a), but

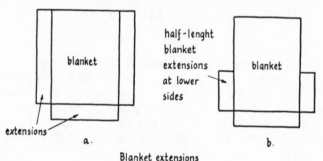

Blanket extensions

65

actually it may be sufficient to have them go only half or a third of the way up (Fig. 65b). If you have traveled in Germany and noticed the extensions that keep the thick, rather narrow "puffs" on the beds, you will know that these short extensions can work very efficiently.

Mending Blanket Holes Machine stitching to mend a hole in a blanket is inadvisable except perhaps near an edge. The close machine stitching will mat down the material, making the blanket a little less warm there. Bring the edges of the hole together with hand stitches, using soft cotton on a cotton blanket and wool yarn on a wool one.

Patches on blankets do not look well at all. Use your ragged blankets for quilt interlinings.

DOLLS_____

The sewing project on which the following suggestions were based was done for the Christmas gift room of our Volunteers for Community Action group.

Christmas Dolls The group of concerned women agreed that all little girls should have dolls for Christmas, if by any means they could be provided. Not enough dolls had been donated that year, so the Volunteers decided to make them.

Four to six ladies, not one of whom considered herself an expert seamstress, craftsman or designer, set out to put together and dress small rag dolls for the 1974 Christmas room. They were far more successful than they had hoped. Even the most crudely made stuffed dolls, when finished and dressed (which always included the underclothes), looked rather attractive. They were placed in the Christmas room and taken home by pleased little girls, or by their mothers for them.

Rag Doll Making The dolls were made by no one pattern or set of directions. Some workers sent for patterns, some copied dolls from books and magazines and some designed their dolls themselves. But each doll was made by a kind and concerned woman who wanted a little girl to be happy with it, and somehow the dolls seemed to carry this message to the little girls.

Until quite lately there was general agreement

that little girls much preferred manufactured dolls. Styles, however, change in dolls as in other things. It is probable that sometime in the future styles in dolls will change again, so anyone planning to make dolls should take warning.

Wigs The mending of body defects, such as tears and eyes needing replacement, was done by youth groups that helped us mend toys. They simply could not mend the wigs.

It was very much worthwhile to make a good wig, for dolls were given to the Volunteers in good condition except for the poor bald heads, and the underprivileged children did so want dolls—the parents would even go into debt to buy them.

Wigs were too expensive to buy; the ordinary price was $2.50 each.

One of our Christmas room chairmen did wonderfully well glueing little tufts of matching "hair" (taken from a sacrificed wig) onto the doll "scalp," pushing the bits up under existing "hair." Another Christmas worker, in desperation, had little bonnets made for the dolls that needed help. Directions come with Raggedy Ann patterns for making yarn loops all around the head. Elaborate purchased outfits for making up dolls of various nationalities have materials and directions for the hair.

Here is the method worked out for making a doll's wig. The wig designed had a center parting and braids down each side of the doll's face.

Clip all the bits of remaining hair off the doll's head. Today's doll ordinarily has the hair inserted into tiny holes all over the scalp, with a double row of holes about the edge of the hairline.

For a scalp to which one can stitch, use the foot of a nylon stocking. Cut it off at the heel and try it on the doll. If it comes to a sort of peak at the toe, take it off, turn it inside out, take it to the sewing machine and stitch across to make a smooth curve, using a fine stitch. Cut off the tip you just stitched out, so that it doesn't make too much of a bunch underneath. Turn the sock right side out and put it on the doll again, adjusting it so that the back seam, if there is any, goes up the exact middle of the back of the head.

Apply a line of fabric cement on the nylon right along the hairline, then work and press the glue through the fine nylon mesh into the line of cut-off hair underneath. (Fig. 66a.) Also, run a line on either side of the central seam, in back. Leave it to dry overnight. You may wish to tie a strip of cloth about the head to hold the glued parts more closely together; if you do this, pull the strip carefully away after about an hour. If necessary, reglue anything that does not seem firm.

Various yarns were tried for hair and worsted worked out best. A medium-fine yarn is needed to cover the scalp yet not make too-large braids.

For a fifteen-inch doll, the total length of the hair across the head and down both braids will be about fifteen inches. Wind your yarn off onto a fifteen-inch strip of cardboard to get this length. Tie it at least twice with bits of string to hold it while you work. Just how many strands you will need will depend at least partly on the size of the yarn you use; the strands should cover the scalp well and be able to make plump braids down beside the doll's face.

Lay the yarn across the top of the doll's head and adjust it so that the length of the two braids will be exactly the same. Pin it in places along the center of the wig; adjust this line with care so that in the back the center line will be on the seam. The yarn is to be stitched from that cemented hairline at the top of the forehead in front to the middle of the neck in back. (Fig. 66b.) All the time you are working, keep

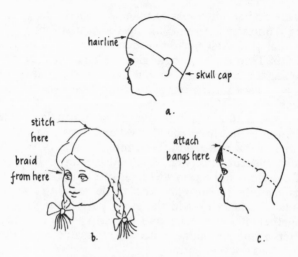

hairline

skull cap

a.

stitch here

braid from here

attach bangs here

b.

c.

Constructing a wig on a doll

66

examining the braids to make sure they stay the same length.

Then, using thread that either is "invisible" or matches the yarn as exactly as possible, sew the yarn to the nylon (that is, the "hair" to the "scalp") along the line of the center part. Use a single running stitch and go back and forth as many times as needed to catch down every strand.

And now you are about done. When you are sure you have the braids the same length, cut through the loops at the bottom. Spread out the yarn carefully from the center part you have just stitched and lay it smooth, with none of the strands overlapping or the wig will not look smooth across the top. Separate the yarn into three strands just above the ears and start braiding from the front. Fasten the ends by wrapping thread about them. If eventually you cover these with ribbons, sew the ribbons in place or they will inevitably come right off and be lost. You will also probably want to hold the braids closer to the doll's face with a bit of cement just above the ears. Again, wrap a strip of cloth about the head to hold the yarn in place until the cement hardens.

If you think that your doll has too high a forehead, make "bangs" from short loops of yarn and sew them in place, above the hairline, before you put the rest of the hair on. They should be somewhat gathered into the middle, not spread along the forehead. Leave the loops uncut until all the rest of the wig is stitched, then clip and trim them. If they stick right out, catch them down with a thin smear of glue across the upper forehead, wrapping the bangs down with a strip of cloth until they dry in place. (Fig. 66c.)

There are many possible variations. Part or all of the back of the scalp may be covered with cloth matching the yarn hair. If this is done, quite heavy yarn, such as rug yarn, can be used and the braids will not be too thick.

Doll Clothes You can use up scraps to make doll underclothes, but choose really pretty material for the doll dresses. When you see, long after, a dress on a grandchild's doll that you once made for her mother's doll, you might wish you had chosen a prettier material from which to make it.

The underclothing and dresses are quite easy to make. (Figs. 67a, b, c, d, e, and 68.) Slight mistakes and miscalculations can be overlooked in doll clothes which would be disastrous in children's or adults' clothing.

All doll clothing now is best made with raglan sleeves and with an opening all the way down the back, for today's dolls usually lack elbow joints and are difficult or impossible to work into too-well-fitted

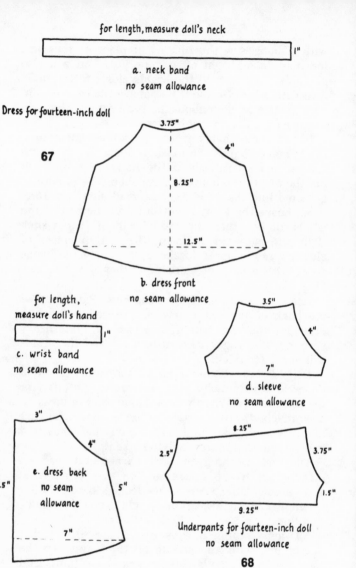

for length, measure doll's neck

a. neck band
no seam allowance

Dress for fourteen-inch doll

67

3.75"

4"

8.25"

12.5"

b. dress front
no seam allowance

for length,
measure doll's hand

1"

c. wrist band
no seam allowance

3.5"

4"

7"

d. sleeve
no seam allowance

3"

4"

8.5"

5"

e. dress back
no seam
allowance

7"

8.25"

2.5"

3.75"

1.5"

9.25"

Underpants for fourteen-inch doll
no seam allowance

68

dresses. Wrap-around petticoats are better, too. The simply cut panties are closed and pulled on, held up by elastic at their tops. Dolls' underclothes are cut the same length, back and front.

Reach into your collection of bits of lace and braid to trim dolls' dresses. A strip down the front from the neckline, of lace, braid or buttons, can look very festive. Lace around the bottom of the panties is just out of this world.

BIAS BINDING————————————————

Bias binding was never really cheap, and with the packets containing fewer and fewer yards of tape it has become relatively expensive.

You can easily cut your own from left-over cloth. Your cloth should be firmly woven and reasonably strong. Medium-weight cotton, already shrunk if possible, with a trace of starch filling for stiffening, will do very well.

Ascertain the "straight of the goods," the line of weaving, each way. If your material shows a selvage, there is one straight edge. If necessary, draw a thread at right angles to the selvage to get the other straight edge. (Fig. 69a.)

Fold your lengthwise straight edge, for which we hope you found a selvage, over the crosswise straight edge, producing a forty-five-degree angle (half a right angle). Crease this fold. (Fig. 69b.) Unfold, lay out on a flat surface and, with a long marker like a yardstick, mark along this fold with a soft-lead pencil or, if you prefer, a chalk sharpened to a point. (Fig. 69c.)

Measure parallels to this line on either side of it of the width you want. The bias binding you buy is usually seven-eighths of an inch wide, and this is a good width to measure off and cut. However, if you know you will be taking in more than two thicknesses of cloth with your binding, a full inch of width may be better. Use a small ruler to mark off the widths in dots or dashes, measuring from both sides from your first diagonal, until you have about the yardage of binding you will need. Mark on the cloth along your yardstick from dot to dot or dash to

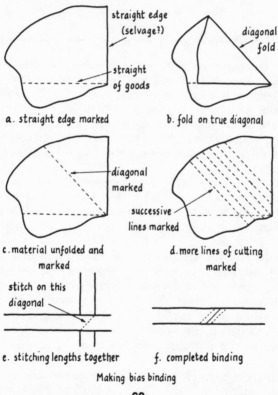

a. straight edge marked

b. fold on true diagonal

c. material unfolded and marked

d. more lines of cutting marked

e. stitching lengths together

f. completed binding

Making bias binding

69

dash, to mark off the strips of binding (Fig. 69d), and cut.

Stitch the lengths together at their ends, diagonally, as was done in the purchased binding. (Figs. 69e, f.)

You will find it a great convenience to have learned to make your own bias binding. Not only is it an economy; you will want sometimes to bind your work with self material or be able to bind it with a pattern or shade of material you cannot find in bias binding in the shops.

FROM DISCARDS_____

Our mending committee included in its work the making over into something else of clothing that was excellent in quality but entirely out of style.

You, too, may find it amusing as well as profitable to try out such "make-overs," so here are directions and observations.

• Hand-Me-Downs

If you wish to make over a not too badly worn garment, perhaps an adult's garment for a child, there are certain elementary precautions you should observe.

Sometimes, especially if you can have some expert or at least experienced help, you can preserve parts of the old garment unchanged, possibly reusing the old collar or the original buttonholes. Rarely can you avoid removing the zipper.

Ordinarily, you would take the old garment entirely to pieces, clean and press them, or have them cleaned and pressed, and then lay out the new pattern on the old pieces.

Then treat the worn garment as you would any "bargain" material you might buy in the shops: look out for the places that are worn, torn, pulled, or badly stained. Search for defects on the right side, then hold the cloth up to the light and look for holes and thin places.

In worn clothing, you examine most carefully the elbows, cuffs and collars of dresses and coats, the knees and seats of pants. But this is not enough; look the piece *all* over. Unless searched for, tiny holes can hide themselves until the parts are cut out and laid in place, or even until you have half finished sewing it. A couple of inches of pulled thread in loosely woven material can spoil the best planned effect.

Take extra care not to use the worn places of an adult's garment in exactly the same location on the child's garment. The worn elbow must not come just at the elbow on the newly made coat. Can't the new elbow be cut from a place a little above and to one side of the old one?

Sometimes a set-in pocket cannot be cut to come exactly where a set-in pocket would belong on the child's coat. But you have a bonus, after all, in this making over; you have extra pieces of unused material from the old garment to make use of. Cut and make up neat patch pockets large enough to cover the visible parts of the former inset pockets and which can also reach over to where patch pockets would belong, to look good, on the newly made garment.

Relax the rule about not buying new cloth for make-overs here. Buy new material to make the new lining.

Worn pants do not make over well. Perhaps you can cut them above the worn knees and use them as shorts. Put large, perfectly obvious matching patches over the worn places on the seats.

• Quilts

Quilts (and blankets) were always the most welcome gifts the Volunteers for Community Action could offer. This seems to be true the world around, whether the quilts and blankets are for refugees far away or for a neighbor of your own who may have lost all in a fire.

Would you like to construct a quilt from left-overs?

A quilt for a double bed should be at least two yards square; a little larger is even better. For a single bed or cot, sixty inches would probably be wide enough. A crib quilt might be a yard by a yard and a half.

For the quilt top, you can use large pieces, as pleated or very full skirts, taken to pieces and pressed out flat. Old-fashioned summer dresses often have full skirts. If they are fairly long skirts, it might take only three of them, across the quilt, to make the top. Some might have to be pieced out.

It is worthwhile, if you can spare the time, to cut smaller wool pieces into large squares and make pieced quilt tops from them. If you can make such tops partly from bright-colored pieces and from plaids, they will make very handsome quilts.

If the quilt top is of wool, you can use old soft cotton goods for the interlining; if the top is of cotton, interline it with woolen things. For any interlinings, see if you can find things that are soft and warm. A great variety of materials can be used, but the first choice, whether the top be of wool or of cotton, is an old blanket. This is a good way to use up quite ragged blankets not worth mending.

For the lining—and experienced quilt makers often call it the "backing," to distinguish it from the interlining—any long-wearing material can be used. Unbleached muslin was a favorite with a previous generation. Today, those who work with welfare recipients ask that, if the lining material is bought especially to line the quilt, bright and pretty cloth be chosen.

Now to start putting it together. Set up your quilting frame, place the lining on it and pin or sew the edges in place. Find the exact midpoint of each side of the lining, as it lies on the frame, and mark this. Lay the interlining on it, piecing it out, if necessary, by laying parts of old flannelette pajamas, etc., over thin or ragged places. Piece out the edges, also, with old soft materials. Don't baste; just lay the pieces in place, overlapping them. (Fig. 70a.) Remember our long-ago forefather's song? "Clouts double, are warmer than single whole clothing."

When you are ready to put it all together, mark the midpoint of each of the four sides of the top. Then, at last, two persons, standing on opposite sides of the frame, lift the quilt top and lower it gently into place on the interlining and lining. Match those midpoint markings. Pin the edges of the top to the lining and to the cloth tacked to or wound around the frame. (Fig. 70b.)

Any quilt made entirely of used materials is hardly worth actual hand quilting. These quilts can be "tied," using cotton string or darning cotton. The placing of the ties can vary from as little as three inches apart when the interlining is much pieced to six inches or more when whole blankets and large pieces of interlining have been available. Sometimes there may be a checked pattern in the top material which can be followed for the tying. Otherwise you would best mark off the positions of the ties with a yardstick, putting in pins, preferably glass-headed, to mark the places. (Fig. 70c.) It is best to use the conspicuous glass-headed pins lest ordinary pins get lost in the quilt.

It is a happy custom, handed down in some

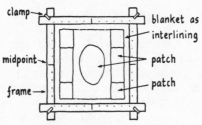

clamp
blanket as interlining
midpoint
patch
frame
patch

a. lining and interlining on frame

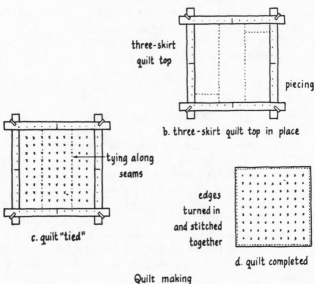

three-skirt quilt top

piecing

b. three-skirt quilt top in place

tying along seams

c. quilt "tied"

edges turned in and stitched together

d. quilt completed

Quilt making

70

families, to tie a short strand, about an inch long, of, usually, bright-colored cotton or artificial yarn (real wool being too expensive, and useful elsewhere) into each knot. A light-colored quilt top with strands of pink and green tied in can look as if sprinkled with apple blossoms.

Turn in the edges and stitch all around the quilt. (Fig. 70d.)

You need a lot of room for a quilt frame as well as space all around it for the worker. Naturally, if a number of persons gather to work on it together, it does not occupy the room for so long. No doubt one reason for the prevalence of quilting parties in olden times was that the housewife could rarely spare the room for the prolonged sessions she would need if she quilted or tied the quilt all by herself.

Wool pieces smaller than pleated skirts can be cut into squares, and they make attractive quilt tops, but it is hardly worthwhile to make pieced quilt tops from used cotton.

• Small Pants

Because pants for five- and six-year-old boys and girls were more in demand than any other garments in the clothing room our inter-church group ran, one of our mending committee members learned to make them. A discarded dress of strong material was her usual source of supply, and corduroy was by far the favorite fabric, as it was warm and could be washed. (Poor folks can't afford dry cleaning.) She made them without pockets or flies, with elastic in the tops, but it is not at all difficult to put in the pockets and the zippered opening. It does take longer, of course.

• Small Underpants

Our committee became locally famous for making men's discarded shirts into girls' underpants. A local welfare worker had begged us to make underpants for poor children, at a time when we had on hand a large quantity of men's white shirts for which hitherto no use had been found.

At the end of several years, over six hundred underpants for small girls from four to eight years (and some for ten- and twelve-year-olds) had been made, mainly from men's shirts. A few had also been made from old summer dresses.

Pattern companies have sets of patterns for girls' underwear containing patterns for slips and more than one pattern for underpants. Use the pattern with the insert in the crotch.

To make them, (Fig. 71) remove the pockets from the shirt. Along the front, carefully remove the buttons and take out any seam there may be next to them. (It is often lock stitched.) On the buttonhole side of the front, cut next to the buttonholes from top to bottom. Use pinking shears for this, even if you have to borrow them. Dampen and press the shirt, ironing the folded edges out flat. Stitch the two sides of the front together. Lay front on back, arrange the pattern on the doubled material and cut the pattern out. (Figs. 71a, b.) The crotch insert can be cut from the top of the back or even from a sleeve (though there is also a way of cutting smaller pants from four sleeves). Obviously, one leg of the underpants will have a seam up the side. (The back of the shirt makes one pant leg; the two sides of the front are stitched together for the other.) By the way, the pattern may be sufficiently old-fashioned to have legs much too long for modern styles. Look

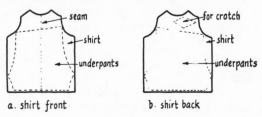

a. shirt front   b. shirt back

71   Underpants from shirt

out for this and take an inch off the lower edge of the pattern, if necessary.

• Scarves and Jumper Dresses

Pleated wool skirts make scarves and jumper dresses. (Plain, dark skirts were used for the quilts; the bright-colored and the plaid ones were saved for scarves and jumpers.) Take all the seams out of the skirts and dampen and press them. For the scarves, cut the strips twelve to fifteen inches wide, more or less according to the width of the skirt you are reusing, of course, and a yard long up to a yard and a half or more, if you can. Stitch all around the edge, as near the edge as you can, and trim the edge to not over a quarter of an inch wide. Then turn a narrow hem and hand hem it. You may like a wool fringe at the ends.

Someone from a family of ski experts protested that long scarves were dangerous, as they get caught on the mechanisms of ski lifts. If the scarves were kept from ski lifts there would be little danger, while long wool scarves folded about your neck (and up about your face when facing the wind) can be very comforting in sub-zero weather.

For the jumper, buy or borrow a pattern, making sure your pattern does not call for material wider or longer than the skirt allows. A pattern with shoulder fastenings is preferable. Use cheerful buttons to fasten it; bright metal ones are especially good.

• Mittens

When a hand-knit sweater or one made on a home knitting machine is too ragged to be worth mending, ravel it out, wash the yarn to get out the kinks and reknit it into mittens. How welcome they are in these cold Vermont winters. Sweaters from Scotland are also sometimes knit so they do not have the raw edges at the seams. They can also usually be raveled into long hanks of yarn, like the homemade sweaters.

• Bootees and Slippers

In the early days of the clothes room, the same concerned social worker who had asked for the underpants for girls suggested a need for slippers for quite small children.

Quite poor people often felt they could hardly afford shoes for preschool children (the Volunteers sometimes raised money to make sure all the older children in the county had shoes and overshoes for school). The social worker knew that floors were often chilly in winter for bare little feet to run about on.

Attractive bootee-slippers can be knitted from odds and ends of yarn. Patterns for these knit bootees direct you to sew up the bottoms of the completed bootees, but bootee-slippers for toddlers should be finished with soles. So omit the four rows of knitting at the very bottom and, instead, stitch the bottom edges to soles. If the slippers are for your own toddler, measure around the foot, or use a small shoe to trace around.

If you have neither toddler foot nor toddler shoe, to make sure you are making your slippers the right size go to a local department store and measure the soles of a pair of slippers marked as being of the size and for the age you want to make the slippers for.

Two-part slipper uppers can be cut from winter coats and their linings from new flannelette. (Figs. 72a, b.) The soles are cut from strong cloth, wool or cotton, with as many thicknesses as can be stitched through on the sewing machine.

Put your thicknesses of sole together and stitch across and back a few times to hold them firmly together. (Fig. 73a.) Put the two upper parts together, right sides together, and stitch from sole to top, front end and back end, and do the same with the linings. (Fig. 73b.) Press the seams open. You now

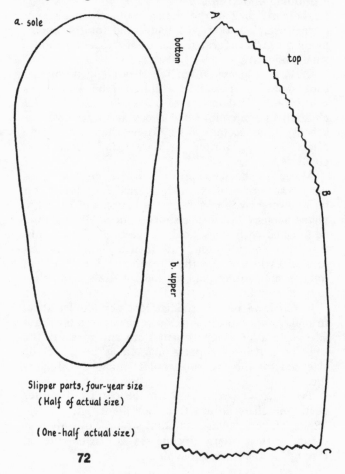

a. sole

bottom

top

A

B

b. upper

D

C

Slipper parts, four-year size
(Half of actual size)

(One-half actual size)

72

have two outside parts and two linings. Baste the tops of the outsides to the tops of the linings, right sides together, and stitch around the joined tops. Turn each right side out. You now have the completed uppers.

Baste them carefully, linings to outsides, around the tops and around the bottoms, which latter are to be stitched to the soles. Stitch or embroider the outsides to the linings around the tops. (Fig. 73c.)

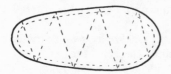

a. sole stitched across

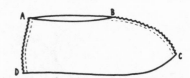

b. uppers stitched, right sides together

c. outside and lining stitched together at top and upper turned right side out

Making toddlers' slippers

73

Now baste the uppers to the soles, taking in the needed fulness about the front ends. You can sew them together with an overcasting stitch, sewing the edges evenly together. Take the slippers to the sewing machine and stitch uppers to soles. Trim the edges.

To strengthen this stitching and improve the appearance of the slippers, put a bias binding, cut at least an inch wide, over this edge stitching. If, however, you find these thicknesses difficult to stitch through, then stitch uppers to soles around twice, trim and finish with an embroidered edge stitch, such as a buttonhole stitch.

Sew a couple of extra thicknesses of lining material right on the inside of the sole, for extra warmth and wear. These extra soles can be made a little smaller than the first sole, to avoid adding to the bulk in the edge stitching. (Fig. 73d.)

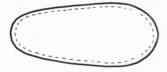

d. sole, inner sole in place

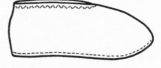

e. completed slipper, side view

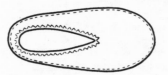

f. completed slipper, top view

Making toddlers' slippers

THE PRAISE OF THE NEEDLE _____

I began this book with a quotation from a poem written in Plymouth, Massachusetts, about 1630.

Let me close with another quotation from the time when mending was an appreciated art. This is from a much-quoted poem, "The Praise of the Needle," written in London, England. The twelfth edition was printed in 1640.

In his praise of the handiwork of the ladies of his time, and in particular of the handiwork of English queens, John Taylor gives us this message:

A Needle (though it be but small and slender)
Yet it is both a maker and a mender:
A graue Reformer of old Rents decayd,
Stops holes and seames, and desperate cuts
    displayd.

May I recommend my book, as John Taylor sagely recommended his: (I copy his spelling as well as his sentiments.)

Thus skilfull, or unskillfull, each may take
This booke, and of it each good use may make.

INDEX——————————————————————